KIDS SAY THE DARNDEST THINGS

KIDS

SAY THE DARNDEST THINGS

Bill Cosby

BANTAM BOOKS

NEW YORK TORONTO LONDON

SYDNEY AUCKLAND

KIDS SAY THE DARNDEST THINGS
A Bantam Book/September 1998

Copyright © 1998 by CBS Worldwide Inc. All rights reserved.

BOOK DESIGN BY GLEN EDELSTEIN

Library of Congress Cataloging-in-Publication Data
Cosby, Bill, 1937–
 Kids say the darndest things / Bill Cosby.
 p. cm.
 ISBN 0-553-11043-8
 1. Children—Quotations. 2. Children—Humor. I. Title.
PN6328.C5C67 1998
081'.083—dc21 98-34141
 CIP

Published simultaneously in the United States and Canada

Bantam Books are published by Bantam Books, a division of Bantam Doubleday Dell
Publishing Group, Inc. Its trademark, consisting of the words "Bantam Books" and
the portrayal of a rooster, is Registered in U.S. Patent and Trademark Office and in
other countries. Marca Registrada. Bantam Books, 1540 Broadway, New York,
New York 10036.

PRINTED IN THE UNITED STATES OF AMERICA

QMB 10 9 8 7 6 5 4 3 2 1

Contents

Preface

In the beginning, there was Art Linkletter, and God saw that Art was good and God said that Art *is* good. A few years after the beginning, there was Cosby, who never argued with God. Cosby knew that Art was an adult with a remarkable hobby: He actually listened to children. He knew that mankind's silliest saying was not *Do not remove this tag from mattress under penalty of law,* but *Children should be seen and not heard,* a tough rule to follow on a television show.

Art knew that adults are just kids who've lost their way, just kids who owe money and who've stopped saying what they really think. And so, Art preferred the wonderfully honest talk of kids, who guilelessly say exactly what's on their minds, even if they don't know what they're saying.

3

Moreover, Art knew a happy truth I also have learned: that the greatest wits who ever lived, from Cyrano de Bergerac to Fat Albert, could never have invented the kind of delightful originality that endlessly bubbles from kids.

"My dad yells at my older brother a lot," a six-year-old girl once told me.

"Why does he have to do that?" I asked her.

"Oh, you know," she said. "He's a *boy*."

"Yes, most brothers are. But why does your dad have to yell at him?"

"Oh, *you* know how *boys* are."

"No, how are they?"

"Stupid."

"And when they become men?"

"Stupider."

Just as I don't argue with God, I don't argue with six-year-old girls because both know more than I do. I just know that the candor of such children is always surprising, sometimes unnerving, and frequently to be treasured.

Moreover, the logic of kids goes far beyond the tiny brain of an adult.

"Mr. Cosby," a six-year-old once said to me, "I know your wife's name."

"Really?" I replied. "What is it?"

"Mrs. Cosby."

Could I have argued with *him*? That kid would have known who is buried in Grant's Tomb. Grant and *Mrs.* Grant. And their son, Cary.

Kids blend logic and creativity into a magnificent mix. For example, I once heard an eight-year-old boy recite this particularly moving passage from the Lord's Prayer: ". . . And lead us not into Penn Station and deliver us from eagles . . ."

Did *Aristotle* have more wisdom? Which of us truly wants to be led into Penn Station, even when the rush hour is over? And would any of us want to be FedExed to eagles, which might deliver *us* somewhere?

By now you're aware that there is a difference between children and old people that has nothing to do with the size of their portfolios. The difference—it's the one big thing Dr. Spock missed—is that kids like to keep their hands in their pockets and old people want you to take them out. When I was five, at least once a day an old person told me to take my hands out of my pockets. You see, in those medieval days, any old person could hit you.

"I brought you into this world," my father used to tell me, "and I can take you out."

Children are as creative with songs as they are with reasons why their hands should stay in their pockets, why they have to put peas in their noses, and why they didn't do it and couldn't have done it and don't know what you're talking about anyway. Who but a child could have collaborated with Stephen Foster to produce the unforgettable new blend of travel and medicine I heard when a five-year-old boy sang to me, "Oh, I come from Alabama with a Band-Aid on my knee."

And he's goin' to Louisiana, his fractured love to see.

The updated version of the Lord's Prayer was the kind of genius I keep hearing from America's shortest wits on my CBS show, *Kids Say the Darndest Things*, the kind that Art Linkletter heard from more than 27,000 kids while running his wondrous *House Party* on radio and TV from 1945 to 1969. The kids I've loved and listened to and laughed with on my show are the grandchildren of the ones who lit up Art Linkletter forty years ago. They're a bit more knowledgeable than Art's: They know that radioactivity isn't a lot of broadcasting, that a free agent isn't a spy on parole, and that a stork who delivered babies would have to bring them through the vaginal canal.

Moreover, most of the kids today, especially the four-year-olds, would probably tell me, "Cosby, don't you real-

ize that kids are now saying the *damndest* things?" How-
ever, no matter what you call them, the things that kids are
saying today are still every bit as funny and original and
wise and ridiculous and absolutely enchanting as ever. Just
listen . . .

Son of Preface

Before we start listening to the darndest things, a few words about the kids, none of whom gave me permission to use their remarks. But I've had such a good time collecting these remarks for you that I don't care if some of the kids turn against society, become lawyers, and sue me. Of course, an attention span of eleven seconds will make law school a challenge for them.

Art Linkletter especially likes the kids who are five and six.

"They don't know what they don't know," he says.

Art and I, on the other hand, are authorities on what we don't know. After all, Art and I both have doctoral degrees, so it is easy for us to be involved in exchanges like this one about what God likes to collect.

Art asked a boy of six, "Do you have any pets?"

"Yes, a dog, but he died."

"Oh, I'm really sorry about that, but at least you know that he's in heaven."

"Why does God want a dead dog?"

Martin Luther stopped asking himself that question and the pope never started. It is a question that could come only from a small child or a large veterinarian. However, the veterinarian's talk would not have the unique quality that Art has nicely described this way: "Kids mix raw truth, incomplete knowledge, preposterous speculation, and pure imagination."

Like the answers on my final exams at Temple; but I was never as entertaining as the small people who have tried to explain the world to Art and me.

In dealing with kids, no matter how little we understand their explanations, we must always remember that *we're* the adults. What this means I have no idea. It certainly means nothing to the kids, who instinctively seem to know that adults are merely strange people who have dopey ideas like "Stop throwing those peas at your sister." The kids know they're not going to eat the peas anyway, so why not use them for a healthy expression of feelings about a sibling while also arranging the peas on the floor for the

dog to eat? The dog might as well enjoy the peas right now, because he is certainly not headed for any Alpo in the sky.

All the kids whom Art and I have struggled to misunderstand on our two shows were between four and twelve. I was between sixty and forty-eight, and Art, like the sphinx, is ageless, though he's much better looking. I was taller than all of the kids, but most of their IQs were higher than mine, even though some of their flies were open.

Needless to say (so why am I saying it?), a lot of the things that kids have said to Art and me through the years were almost as forgettable as most of what we have heard from adults. But then there were the gems, the brightest of which are in this book, where you will hear voices that spoke before being dulled by the censor of maturity. In the jewelry store you are entering, candor is constantly being redefined by people who would tell you that candor is a California bird. Kids are simply the best things any of us will ever know. Remember: "The emperor has no clothes" wasn't spoken by his tailor.

In the tradition of Art's *House Party,* the kids on my show never knew what I was going to say, but such knowledge would have been meaningless because the

best things they said were non sequiturs. And even the *sequiturs* didn't follow so well—in the scheme of adult logic, that is. Kids have their own logic, a kind that might have made Socrates go for the hemlock much sooner. For example, consider the philosophy of the young woman—I think she was eight—with whom I had this exchange:

"When you grow up, how many children would you like to have?" I asked.

"About three or four. Or maybe ten."

"And what kind of husband would you like?"

"Oh, I don't want no husband."

This young lady, like the lad who understood the unpromising afterlife for a basset hound, knew something that transcended both convention and grammar, something no adult could ever understand. Yes, kids are mystically wise and also passionately honest—except when they're lying.

The wonderful honesty of kids could not be better captured than it was in a letter that my daughter Erika received one day when she was staying out of school because she had the measles. All of Erika's second-grade classmates wrote letters to her, but none more eloquent than this:

KIDS SAY THE DARNDEST THINGS

DEAR ERIKA:

I hope you get well soon.
Mrs. Dickey forced us to write this letter. So I'm
not writing it because I like you.

> Your friend,
>
> Leon

Although everything said to me on *Kids Say the Darndest Things* was spontaneous, the kids had been coached for weeks by their parents, all of whom seemed eager to prevent national humiliation. This coaching, of course, was pointless, because the last kid who listened to his parents lived in 1293. They told him to clean up his room or they would feed him to a dragon.

"After you feed me, could I have it for a pet?" he replied.

1.

Devout Darlings

A kid may not know where he left his homework or right shoe, but he knows the Bible, perhaps because he spends so much time praying that his mother won't find the new stain on her rug, which could have come from *anyone* who happened to drop a glass of grape juice there. It wasn't *his* fault that she put the rug there, and maybe God will explain that to her.

On both of our shows, Art Linkletter and I have discovered this deeply religious feeling in kids. After all, doesn't the Bible say: "And a little child shall mislead them?"

———

"Do you know what Easter is?" I asked one girl of five.

"Oh, yes," she replied. "Easter is when Jesus died and they put Him in a tomb with a big rock and then three days

19

later they rolled back the rock and Jesus walked out and He didn't see His shadow."

Which meant that the Holy Land would have six more weeks of winter.

Kids may be weak on Matthew, Mark, Luke, and John, but they are all experts on Genesis, probably because it's a rock band.

"Do you know the story of Adam and Eve?" I said to one six-year-old girl.

"*Everyone* knows that story," she replied.

"Well, who made Adam?"

"God."

"And who made Eve?"

"Eve was made out of a rib."

"Yes, but it was a special *kind* of rib."

"A chicken rib."

The Gospel according to Colonel Sanders. Not everyone, of course, believes that Eve was made from a chicken rib. Certain denominations believe that she was made from a thigh, but this is no place to get into a debate about how many angels can stand on a wishbone.

KIDS SAY THE DARNDEST THINGS

It is always heartening to see kids using the Bible as a guide to good behavior.

"Do you try to do the things that Jesus told you to do?" I asked a boy of nine named Peter.

"He didn't tell me to do nothin'," Peter fervently replied.

"I mean things like turning the other cheek."

"What's that mean?"

"If somebody hits you, you don't hit him back."

"Jesus said be a wimp?"

"No, not a wimp, a lover of peace."

"It don't sound too smart. Why don't the guy who hits me love peace *first*?"

"Well, that's the whole point of Jesus' message: You have to be *bigger* than the other person."

For a moment, Peter fell into reverent reflection.

"If you're bigger," he then said, "you should definitely hit him back."

Not *all* Peters are saints.

———

In talking to very young people, I have gained insights into the Bible that you will not get in divinity school, unless you're majoring in exorcism.

"Do you know what happened to Adam and Eve in the Bible?" I asked one seven-year-old boy.

Bill Cosby

"Sure," he said. "They ate the apple and then God told them to get out of the Garden of Even, so they went to the airport."

The Garden of Even, of course, is not to be confused with the Garden of Odds, a place in a different desert where I have done a considerable amount of praying.

"I'm not sure they went to the airport," I told him, "because airports hadn't been invented yet."

I know my history.

"Well," he said, "that's how they got out of town when God told them they had to move."

The Bible is full of miracles, and this clearly was the first one: The evicted couple taking El Al to a new neighborhood, where Eve knew that having a baby wouldn't be a lot of laughs.

————

Yes, children have an understanding of the Bible that can only be called mystical.

"Do you know how God punished Adam and Eve for eating the apple?" I asked one small boy whose name was Max.

"Yeah," he replied. "God made 'em sit down and read the Bible."

22

"Well, at *that* point, reading the Bible didn't take very long."

"No, the Bible's a *big* book. They got 'em in church. I see 'em there all the time."

"What I mean, Max, is that almost nothing had *happened* yet when they were in the Garden of Eden, so there was almost nothing to *put* in the Bible."

"Maybe in *your* church," said Max.

As theologians have always known, the story of Adam and Eve is open to many interpretations, particularly by people under eight.

"What's your favorite Bible story?" I asked a young lady named Maria.

"Adam and Eve," she said.

"How does that one go?" I said, as if I didn't know. When talking to kids, you've got to pretend you don't know much—and a few seconds later, you realize you're not pretending. As Dr. Seuss said, "An adult is an obsolete child."

"Well, first God made Adam," said Maria.

"And how did He do that?"

"Outa stuff He had lying around."

"You mean stuff in a kind of workshop in the sky? A kind of heavenly Home Depot?"

"He's *God*. He can *do* that kind of thing."

"Of course; I'll keep that in mind. And so how did God then make Eve?"

"Out of a rib."

A return to the main menu.

"What kind of rib?" I said.

"A rare rib."

"A *spare* rib?"

"No, a *rare* rib."

"But of course, it was really a *spare* rib too."

"*Huh?*"

Huh? was perhaps the right thing to say to a man whose monologue about Noah was a contribution to biblical scholarship that is not yet an elective in divinity schools.

"Did you ever read the Bible?" I asked another very young man.

"A little," he replied. "But I've heard your record about Noah."

"You *have?*"

"Yeah, my dad made me hear it."

"And what did you *think* of it?"

"It was okay."

"You liked it that much. Well, part of the Bible is based on that record."

"I didn't know that."

"Most people don't. It's the part about Noah. Do you know what happened to Noah?"

"Yeah, he took all the animals and built an ark and then it rained a lot for a few years and then it cleared up."

"Must have been El Niño. So what happened to the animals?"

"They put 'em in a zoo."

"There were *zoos* in those days?"

"Don't you know that?"

I used to know a *lot:* my brain peaked right after I left graduate school; but then I started talking to kids and now I'm not sure of my address. For example, listen to the mental deprogramming I had when I talked to another young biblical scholar on *Kids Say the Darndest Things.*

"What faith are you?" I asked him.

"What's a faith?" he said.

"What religion?"

"Oh, Jewish, but we don't always go."

"Go where?"

"To the Jewish place."

"You mean the synagogue."

"Whatever."

What moving devotion from this tentative part of a great religion that would survive even him. Five thousand years ago, King Solomon, upon arising each morning, must have said, "Let us go now to the whatever."

Eager to explore more of the Old Testament with this sometime scholar, I said, "Do you know what the Torah is?"

"Oh, sure," he said, and I braced myself for him telling me that "Torah! Torah! Torah!" is what the pilots cried as they bombed Pearl Harbor.

"And what's your favorite part of the Torah?" I said.

"My favorite part is when God made America."

———

Although kids are certainly aware of the principle of the separation of church and state, a lot of them still feel that God made America, and Barbados too. After all, Irving Berlin didn't write "God Bless Greece." Yes, every kid finds comfort in knowing that God is an American; and we're mighty proud to have Him too.

A good friend of mine is a Jewish writer who enrolled his six-year-old daughter, Lori, in the kindergarten of Stu-

art Country Day School of the Sacred Heart, probably because he wanted to hedge his salvational bets. When Lori returned from her first day of school, my friend said, "Well, how was it?"

"Fine, Daddy," she replied. "And you'll be proud of me. I didn't say the Pledge of Allegiance."

"Why not?"

"Because I'm Jewish. We don't have allegiance. Only Catholics do, right?"

"No, honey, allegiance isn't one of their holidays. Neither is allowance."

————

My friend's daughter had the same Zen view of religion held by so many of the wee faithful who have enlightened Art and me.

"Do you know why we give thanks at Thanksgiving?" my friend once asked her.

"Because that's when Pharaoh passed over the Pilgrims," she replied.

————

Devoutly divergent is what they all are.

"Tell me, what is heaven like?" I asked one girl of five on the show.

"Like California," she replied.

"And what's hell like?"

"Philadelphia."

———

Again, I didn't want to argue with a child, but Philadelphia is closer to the wrong side of purgatory. I happened to have spent considerable time in prayer in Philadelphia when I was growing up there—or *trying* to grow up. I used to pray that my father wouldn't find me during those moments when he told my mother tenderly, "When I find him, I'm gonna break him in two."

"Why would you want *twice* as many?" my mother would reply.

Those were the days before child abuse. You simply got hit from time to time, but there was no 800 number you could call.

———

My mention of that number reminds me of the boy of six who asked me if there was an address for the Garden of Eden.

"I think it was way out of town," I said. "By the way, do you know what happened to Adam and Eve in the Garden?"

"Yes," he said. "They ate the apple and went to hell and their parents went to Los Angeles."

It might have been hell for the parents too, in Los Angeles without a car.

————

Art Linkletter lives in Los Angeles with a car but without a clue as to what any kid is going to say, the same clue that has never come to me.

One day on his show, Art asked a girl of seven, "What's your favorite Bible story?"

"David and Goliath," she replied.

"What happened in that one?"

"David cut off the lion's head."

"Are you sure that wasn't *Daniel* who got involved with the lion?"

"Who's Daniel?"

"My accountant. I guess I'm thinking of another story."

"You're all mixed up."

"Okay, I think I've got it now: David cut off the lion's head. And what does that teach us?"

"Don't lose your head."

————

Art, however, ignored this ancient wisdom, because he continued to ask the same question, as if the answers would make sense.

"What's *your* favorite Bible story?" he asked someone posing as a boy of seven.

"Noah and the Ark," the person said.

"And you know what Noah took into the ark?" said Art, expecting the boy to say, "His flood insurance policy."

"Yeah, two kinds of animals, except hamsters."

"And why didn't he take those?"

" 'Cause they wasn't invented."

Art was, of course, too gracious to correct the boy and tell him, "No, 'cause they *weren't* invented."

———————

The story of Noah is open to many different interpretations by kids, depending on their ages, their denominations, and the number of gerbils they have.

"What did Noah do?" I asked one girl, who was six.

"He collected a lot of animals," she replied.

"That was his hobby?"

"Yeah."

"But didn't he have a *special* collection?"

"Yeah, Bible animals."

"It was two of each, right?"

"You know the story?"

"I do."

"So why are you asking me?"

"Well, that's sort of my job on this show. And tell me, do you know *why* Noah took in two kinds of animals?"

"To keep 'em from getting bored."

A fascinating thought: Do animals get bored? Is there a cocker spaniel who feels he'll go mad if he has to retrieve one more slipper? Is there a cow who feels there has to be more to life than just lactating at five in the morning? Is there a mosquito who feels that sucking blood has lost its special kick? Only a child can make us see such things, no matter how much we would rather not.

———

My understanding of the Bible was enriched when I asked another girl of six, "And what's *your* favorite Bible story, Jill?"

" 'The Three Little Pigs,' " Jill replied.

Yes, one of St. Paul's finest letters to the Corinthians, who had asked him about pork futures. I have always preferred that Bible story to the story of Goldilocks and the three Babylonians.

———

"My favorite Bible story," said Sam, who was eight, "is the rich man and the poor man."

"Is that the one where Jesus drives the moneylenders from the temple?" I asked him.

"There was no *cars* for Jesus," he said, looking at me as if wondering how a man so dim had been able to get his own TV show. "Cars wasn't invented in the olden days."

"Of course; I must have been thinking of a different temple, one in Beverly Hills." Never tell a child the wrong date for an invention, whether a hamster or a Toyota; every child is a walking patent office.

"So what happened with the rich man and the poor man?" I said.

"Well, the poor man keeps begging the rich man for money," said Sam, "but the rich man only gives him a penny."

"And what do we learn from that?"

"That the rich man goes to hell."

Where he is safe from the IRS because he deducted ten thousand dollars for charity.

———

Perhaps the most winged thoughts about the Bible I ever received came from a girl of five named Judy.

"Can you tell me the story of Adam and Eve?" I asked her.

"Sure," Judy said. "You see, God made Adam and Adam made Eve and then they had a snake."

"You mean they had a pet?"

"Yeah, but he was a *terrible* pet."

"They should've had a dog."

"Right. And this snake, he told 'em to have apples for dinner, but God didn't want 'em to have dinner, so He got mad and gave 'em a punishment."

"And what was the punishment?"

"That Eve had a whole mess o' babies."

Has there ever been a better description of the human race?

———————

Kids are as creative in interpreting the New Testament as they are with the Old.

"What's your favorite Bible story?" I asked a young lady of seven.

"The trick Jesus did at that wedding," she said.

"You mean when He turned water into wine?"

"Yeah, what a trick! That's better'n pouring water down your pants only they don't get wet."

"Jesus couldn't do that one 'cause pants hadn't been invented yet." (I took a shot.) "So tell me, what does that trick at the wedding teach us?"

"The more wine you get, the better the wedding is."

I've been at weddings where Jesus would have wanted to turn the wine into water.

———

On another show, a young lady of eight gave me a new insight into Holy Week.

"What's Good Friday?" I asked her.

"That means there's no school the next day," she replied.

I believe a minister did once tell me about the meaning of Slugabed Saturday.

———

One of the most entertaining things about kids is that they see all human history as something that happened last weekend, from Good Friday to Swell Sunday. For example, I said to one girl of nine, "What's your favorite Bible story?"

"Abraham and Lot," she replied.

"What happened?"

"Well, they were fighting over money."

"There was money in those days?" I said, wondering about the rate of exchange east of Eden.

"Yeah, a lot of it."

"So what finally happened with Abraham and Lot?"

"They put a check in the Bank of America."

Some kids, of course, think it was First Galilee Trust, for most kids are certain that banks are older than the misguided historians have said. In fact, the average eight-year-old knows that the West Bank is a branch of Chase Messiah.

Kids also have an original view of the denominations of animals. To us ignorant adults, animals aren't too involved in Passover, Christmas, or Lent. However, a very young lady named Molly, daughter of my literary agent, knows differently. After taking her to the American Museum of Natural History one day, her father said, "Would you like to go to the Jewish Museum next?"

"What's there?" said Molly. "Jewish dinosaurs?"

———

Long before I began studying theology with seven-year-olds, Art Linkletter was attending the same school: the semi-seminary.

"Do you know what Adam and Eve wore?" said Art to one boy of seven on *House Party*.

"To what?" the boy replied.

Bill Cosby

"Well . . . when they went on a picnic with Abel and Cain. What kind of clothes did they wear?"

"Oh, they only wore figments."

Art told me he's been looking for a nice lightweight summer figment, but very few stores carry a first-rate line of invisible clothing.

———

A dapper dresser, Art has always been particularly interested in Sinai suits.

"Do you know the story of Joseph and his coat?" he asked a girl of six on his show.

"Well," she said, "Joseph didn't wear bathrobes like all the other men in the Bible. He liked sports coats and he had one of many colors."

"I've been wondering about getting one of those too," Art told me. "But I'm tall and the girl didn't tell me how many colors would work for my height. Also, a blue-green-yellow-brown-orange jacket may have looked better on Joseph, who was a thirty-two short."

———

Art and I have both felt a little extinct when we've explored the Bible with people whose bodies are smaller than ours but whose brains are definitely not.

KIDS SAY THE DARNDEST THINGS

One day on *House Party,* Art asked an eight-year-old boy, "Do you know where Pharaoh's daughter found Moses?"

"In the bullfight," the boy replied, knowing that Moses had been born in Mexico City.

"And what happened to him then?" Art foolishly asked.

"Look," he said, "that was a long time ago. I don't remember."

———

Art and I, of course, remember. As the kids might say, we're the middle ages.

On another of his shows, Art explored the status of royalty in Moses' time.

"Pharaoh was sort of the king of Egypt, right?" he said to a girl of seven.

"No, he was the pharaoh," she replied.

Art should have realized the difference. After all, there was no such thing as Martin Luther Pharaoh.

"And do you know what Pharaoh means?" he asked her.

"He runs the country and plagues and stuff like that," she said.

"You know, Moses' own country, Israel, was soon run by kings too."

"*All* countries are run by kings, queens, and jacks."

37

"Yes, of course," said Art at the end of this hand of Bible-is-wild.

———

Years before, when God had chosen Art to be the officially bewildered straight man for kids, he had learned to listen to the kids not just with affection but also with awe. He once had asked a ten-year-old boy what it meant to write a story in the first person.

"That means writing it like Adam would," the boy said.

Would a story in the third person mean writing it like Abel or writing it like Cain?

———

During my own years with all the short people who kept talking over my head, my richest moment of biblical education came when I asked a gentleman of nine, "What are the Ten Commandments?" I had expected him to tell me about freedom of speech and habeas corpus and the right not to testify against yourself to the principal, but he surprised me. No, actually he *didn't:* When talking to kids, the only surprise is an answer you expect.

"The First Commandment is: Boys can't wear their hair like girls," he said.

Good grooming was important to God from the very

beginning; and He accepted no excuses, such as saying the Sinai was out of rinse.

"And the second one?" I fearlessly said.

"Boys are not supposed to be mad at girls," he said.

"Can girls get mad at *boys*?"

"Why not?"

Art, things have been divinely stacked against us from the beginning.

"And what's the Third Commandment?"

"I forget."

It was probably about curfew on school nights. You couldn't take out the camel after nine.

"So you don't know any more?" I said.

"No, I know the fourth," he said. "The fourth is: God can't trust us."

No Mensa meeting will ever hear a more cosmic truth.

"I'm afraid that's very true: God *can't* trust us."

"You too."

"*I* can't trust us?"

"No, God can't trust you."

"I'll have to talk to Him about that. Okay, what's the Fifth Commandment?"

"People are not supposed to watch TV in their parents' room."

If there has *ever* been an ancient ethical problem, it is

people viewing TV in the wrong rooms. And in parts of
Mesopotamia, they used to steal the remote.

"And the sixth?" I asked him.

"Girls can't cut their hair," he said.

He was giving me tablets of *Vogue.*

"Where did you learn these commandments?" I said.

"*Everyone* knows them," he told me. "And the eighth
is—"

"You skipped the seventh."

"I'll come back to that. The eighth is: Boys can't hit girls.
The ninth is: Girls have to be quiet."

"We'll have to push *that* one harder in church," I said.
"And the tenth?"

"My mom isn't supposed to make me clean up my
room."

The Crusades were fought for *that* one.

———

No matter what denomination a child may be, he still likes
to be a holy free agent.

"Do you like Christmas?" I asked one boy.

"Yeah," he said, "but I'm changing. My friend Harry's
gonna let me be Jewish."

"Is he a rabbi?"

"No, he's just a kid. Whaddaya mean?"

I've been asked this question more than once. Adults don't always understand me either.

"What I mean is: Why are you changing from Christian to Jewish?"

"Because you get a present every night of the week for Harmonica."

If he had changed to African American, he could have celebrated Mario Lanza.

————

Perhaps the most creative interpretation of religion on *Kids Say the Darndest Things* came from a girl of five who visited the show to enrich my spirituality.

"What is your favorite hymn?" I asked her.

" 'Come and Rain over Us,' " she replied.

"You mean 'Come Thou Almighty King.' "

"That one too."

"Why do you like it so much?"

"Because I like the rain. I like to hear it go splish-splash."

" 'Splish-Splash' was by Bobby Darin. The reign in that song is not the kind that goes splish-splash. It's a different kind of reign."

"There's more than one kind?"

"Yes, there's the kind that falls from the sky and there's

the kind that means a king is ruling and there's the kind that holds a horse."

For about five seconds, she looked at me the way a microbiologist looks at a rare disease. And then she spoke the seven words that have summed up a kid's view of adults since the first pharaoh rolled the first Easter eggs: "I don't know what you're talking about."

————

In the matter of not understanding what is being discussed, a subject in which both Art Linkletter and I are international authorities, three years ago I had a brief theological seminar with a boy of seven named David, and I am still trying to figure out his final thought.

"What's your favorite Bible story?" I asked him.

"Adam and Eve," David replied.

"Tell me about it," I said, ready for the story of either Adam and Eve or Ben and Jerry.

"Well, first there was God," he said, and that much was right: There *was* God before Art Linkletter. "And then God made Adam and Eve out of dust."

"And so, when God punished them, he was the first Dustbuster?" I said.

"*Huh?*"

"Sorry, I was just having some fun." At least, *one* of us was. "You go right ahead, David."

"So God put Adam to sleep."

"And then what happened?"

"Then God went to see somebody."

Now, here's what I forgot to ask David: How could God go to see somebody when there was nobody else around?

And David no doubt would have cleared up my confusion by explaining, "I don't know what you're talking about."

————

In my theological conversations with kids, I have discovered that they know more about religion than just what is almost in the Bible. While talking to a boy of nine named Raymond, I made the mistake of mentioning Michelangelo's immortal ceiling in the Sistine Chapel in Rome.

"Did you ever hear of an artist named Michelangelo?" I asked him.

"Michael who?" Raymond replied.

"Michelangelo. That was his whole first name."

"He had another one after *that?*"

"Yes, and I really don't know why. At any rate, he was so inspired by the Bible that he painted the whole story of

creation on the ceiling of a chapel in Vatican City. You know where that is?"

"In Canada?"

"Close, in Rome."

"That's kinda crazy."

"That Vatican City's not in Canada?"

"No, I mean painting stuff on the ceiling. Why didn't he put it on the *walls*? You can see 'em better."

"Maybe he wasn't a genius, after all."

"Well, I never heard of him."

"But now you have. And now you know what the Sistine Chapel is."

"Why'd they need so many of 'em?" said Raymond.

"So many what?" I said, wondering if there would be a spot where I could join this conversation.

"Why'd they need sixteen chapels? Did Mike Angelo paint 'em *all*?"

These were cosmic questions, of course, as was: Did the chapel get its name because *Sixteen Candles* was filmed there? But perhaps the greatest question of all was: Why hadn't I talked to Raymond about Michael Jordan instead?

2.

Beloved Foes

The heart of America is the family, for the family is what shapes kids into the befuddled adults they become, into the people who can't wait to tell psychiatrists about their families. On one of his *House Party* shows, Art Linkletter was given a look at American family life that should have been captured by Norman Rockwell. Well, Norman Schwarzkopf perhaps.

"You're from a big family, I hear," said Art to a boy who was seven.

"Right," he said. "Six kids."

"Counting you."

"No, that's seven."

"And I hear you live in a house that has just one bathtub and one heater."

"Right."

"How does that work out?"

"Well, every week when it's time to take a bath, my dad lines us all up on the lawn outside and then he blows a whistle and we race to the tub. The first one to get there takes the first bath and then the second and the third, like that."

"You really like a hot bath, eh?"

"I don't know. I've never had one."

———

This young man, a filthy part of a fleet-footed family, probably had the same feeling about his siblings as a boy of six to whom I talked on my show.

"What's the best present you ever got?" I asked him.

"A skateboard," he said.

"And what was the worst?"

"My sister," he movingly replied.

———

Many kids would like to see siblings come the way skateboards do: so you can roll them away.

"Do you have any brothers or sisters?" I asked one girl of five.

"I have a new baby brother," she said, "but maybe not for long."

"He's getting married?" I said.

"No," she told me, "we may give him back."

Bursting with family feeling, this young woman felt that it would be nice if her mother returned that baby for hospital credit, on a face-lift perhaps.

What parents never realize is that their kids are little X-ray machines that see deeply into their minds and hearts and checkbooks too.

"What does your father do?" I asked one five-year-old boy.

"He's a fund-raiser," the boy replied.

"For whom does he raise funds?"

"Himself."

I wonder if this boy will be grounded for the audit.

In discussing their parents, other kids are more discreet than this little stoolie.

"Who's the boss of your house?" said Art Linkletter to one six-year-old girl. "Your mother or your dad?"

"Both of them," she replied.

"Say, you're a diplomat."

"No, I'm a Methodist."

Right *there* is the genius of kids: Not only do their answers sometimes have no relation to the questions, they have no relation to *anything*.

———

Other times, however, these small people achieve Socratic wisdom.

"Does your mother pick you up at school?" I asked one boy of eight.

"Oh, sure," he replied.

"And you like that."

"Oh, sure."

"*Why* do you like that?"

"So I don't have to walk home."

You don't need a doctoral degree to figure that one out. I *have* a doctoral degree and it's worthless when children are talking down to me.

———

Mothers not only save their kids from having to walk home from school, they also give their kids the social polish that allows them to dine outside of a cage.

"What are the most important table manners that your mother has taught you?" I asked a boy of seven.

"Don't throw rolls at your sister," he cheerfully replied.

"Oh, yes, that's a good one, especially important for cotillions."

"Throw peas," he said.

"Yes, they *would* be easier on your sister—unless they're frozen, of course."

"And there's a lot more of 'em."

"Something that every ambassador should remember. Are there any other manners that are particularly important to your mom?"

"Don't throw food under the table unless there's an animal there 'cause it'll go bad. And swallow all your food."

"Instead of spitting it out," I said.

"No, before you start talking. And don't wipe your mouth on your sleeve."

"You'd be surprised how often I forget that one. I try to dine in T-shirts so I don't slip."

"You're just foolin' around, right?"

"But never at the table. I always made sure I had said 'Excuse me' before I started throwing things at my brother."

No matter how passionately adults coach kids not to use entrees as ammunition, no adult could ever coach the kids on these shows, though Art and I would have accepted help.

On one show, I asked a boy of five, "What did your parents tell you about coming on the show?"

"To keep my zipper up," he replied.

Pretty good advice for young women too.

────────

One thing about me: I spend a lot of time at colleges, but I still never learn, for I posed the same question to another boy.

"Did your parents give you any advice about how to behave on this show?" I said.

"Yes," he said. "Not to make my mother look like a jackass."

But she didn't have to worry: The kids never do that to their mothers. They are too busy working on me.

────────

And once more, on another show, I asked a girl of five, "Did your mother tell you anything about what to say today?"

"Yes, not to say she's fifty," the young woman replied.

"What a lovely relationship you and your mother used to have."

Now you can see why the CIA doesn't use children. They start *off* as double agents.

————

Art Linkletter also made the mistake of asking some of the kids if their parents had given them any orders about the way to behave on the show.

"My mother told me not to be funny," one girl of six said to him, "because that's what you get paid for."

I wonder if Art's wife, Lois, ever said to him, "Be funnier or they'll start paying the kids."

————

On another *House Party,* a boy of seven said to Art, "My mother told me to pay no attention to whatever my father said to me."

American fathers are like members of the British House of Lords: They have a certain ceremonial air, but no one is required to pay attention to anything they say. And they also spend a lot of time in their robes.

This ancient principle was confirmed on one of my

shows when I asked a boy of eight, "What do you think is the one thing in the world that your father needs most?"

"Sleep," he replied.

————

So many kids see their fathers as men who are seeking unconsciousness.

"What do you think your daddy does best?" I asked one young man of five.

"Fall asleep in the chair," he replied.

————

On one *House Party* show, Art discovered a father who did one particular thing better than any father who ever lived.

"My dad's a lawyer," said a girl of six to Art, "but he's learning to do something else."

"What else?"

"Have a baby."

"Well," said Art, deeply impressed by this offbeat sharing of roles, "that's really a change of pace for *any* man. What does your *mother* say about it?"

"It was her idea."

"Really?"

"Yes, she said if there was going to be another baby in the family, *he'd* have to have it."

Any kid will tell you that mothers have *all* the ideas.

To a boy of six, I once said, "When you're in trouble, which parent would you go to?"

"I'd go to my father," the boy replied, "because he'd have to get permission from my mother to punish me."

Fatherhood redefines ceremonial office.

While fathers are pleasant figureheads, there is a special bond between children and their mothers.

"Do you help your mother clean up the house?" I asked one girl of seven.

"No," she sweetly replied, "I help make the mess."

It's a dirty job, but *somebody's* got to do it.

Mothers know the secret of exercising authority, but fathers have never been able to get clearance for such classified information. The eternal struggle of the American father to make his presence felt can reach piteous proportions.

For example, one recent morning, I overheard this poignant exchange between a father and his five-year-old son.

"I want my lunch," the boy proclaimed.

55

To which his father replied, "Well, how do you *ask* for it?"

"Like this: *I want my lunch.*"

The father, of course, wanted manners. However, being a man, and therefore copeless, he had asked his question as if he wanted a clarification of a sentence that contained four one-syllable words. Fathers are always falling into such untenable positions. The only way we can avoid them is to pursue our favorite pastime and go to sleep.

———

Had he been asleep, a literary friend of mine would not have been able to enjoy the following philosophical exchange with one of his daughters that began when he said, "Honey, your sister told me you stepped on her face while she was lying on the rug. Did you really do that?"

"Well, that's *her* story," his beloved daughter responded.

"Is it true?"

"Well, *maybe*—but there's a good *reason.*"

"A good *reason*?"

"Because I hate her guts."

"But sisters shouldn't feel that way about each other.

56

Look, why not just *talk* to her instead of trying to rearrange her face?"

"Daddy, how can I talk to people I hate?"

Most of the world's peace conferences fail because the delegates ignore that question.

———

If a father went to sleep *before* his children, then he would not have to play the rewarding scene that I once played with my youngest daughter.

"Honey, how about getting into your pajamas?" I tentatively said to her, half hoping she wouldn't hear me.

"Any special reason?" she replied.

"Yes, you're going to bed."

"But *why*?"

"Because that's what children do," I said, flaunting my quickness of mind.

"No one *else* is in bed at eight o'clock."

"Nonsense. Millions of children are—and don't ask for names."

"But *why* do I have to go to bed?"

"Because you have a lot of playing to do tomorrow."

"I'll do some of it now. Then I won't have so much to do tomorrow."

And I should have said: "And I'll be more ineffective now. Then I won't have to be it so much tomorrow."

————————

With my daughter, I'd been haplessly trying to follow the wisdom of my own mother, who had told me, "It's the sleep before midnight that counts." For years, I pondered this potential truth: A child must have eight hours of sleep every night; but if sleep after midnight doesn't count, then a child has to go to bed at four in the afternoon. Luckily, the matter became academic, for my children carried on my own tradition of ignoring all parental advice.

————————

Children are often wiser than my mother; they are often wise beyond their years. Of course, when your years are five, that isn't too hard to be wise beyond. Some kids, however, are think-tank material.

"What would you like to be when you grow up?" said Art Linkletter to one girl of seven.

"A nurse," she replied.

"All right," said Art, "suppose I come into your office with a high fever and dizziness and chills. What would you say to me?"

"Sit down, it'll be an hour wait."

And during that hour, she would find time to say, "The doctor doesn't take assignment." We hope she would say it before the patient slipped into unconsciousness.

Beside her in that think tank will be the five-year-old to whom Art once said, "What do you want to be when you grow up?"

"Alive," the boy replied.

Is there a *second* choice?

In *charge* of the think tank will be a boy who was only four when Art asked him, "What do you want to be when you grow up?"

"I don't want to be anything," the boy replied.

"Don't you want to get married?"

"If I have to."

"And how will you get money?"

"My wife can work."

"But suppose she won't?"

"I'll send for my mother."

That's how shrewdly kids think: Don't go through the

headache of taking out a bank loan; send for your mother. She'll never think of running a credit check.

———

I heard such refreshing honesty from a boy of six on one of my shows.

"What's the first thing you think of when you wake up in the morning?" I asked him.

"Going to the bathroom," he said.

"And what's the last thing you think of in bed at night?"

"Going to the bathroom."

His entire day was framed urologically.

———

Children between five and ten are particularly honest in thinking about their careers; and the five-and-ten is where they don't want to work, whether or not it exists.

On one of my shows, I asked a boy of seven named Brian, "What do you want to be when you grow up?"

"A psychiatrist," Brian replied.

"And why do you want to be a psychiatrist?"

"Because then when you get mad at somebody, you can put them away."

Precisely why Mrs. Freud was always especially nice to the man.

KIDS SAY THE DARNDEST THINGS

———

Yes, kids are in awe of power, whether psychiatric or presidential; it's the parental kind that doesn't impress them.

"What is the president's job?" I asked a girl named Judy, who was eight.

"To make the world better," she replied.

"And what's his wife's job?"

"To make *him* better."

I was about to ask Judy why the president's wife didn't just skip over the middleman and go directly to work on the world, but she quickly added, "You see, sometimes he doesn't feel so good."

"Maybe she should call the Psychic Network."

"Oh, he doesn't need a psychiatrist," she said.

———

Children have their own psychic networks in which adults uneasily live.

"Do you think there's life in outer space?" I once asked a boy of seven.

"Sure, *I'm* an alien," he replied.

Maybe he wasn't seven but six hundred.

"Where are you from?" I asked him.

"Downtown Mars," he said.

"Do you know the zip code?"

"There's no zip codes on *Mars*," he said, looking at me as if I were spacey myself.

"And tell me, why have you come all the way to Earth?"

"For a vacation."

"You must've had frequent flier miles. I know Martians come down here to invade us from time to time, but do many come for vacations?"

"Yeah, they like Miami Beach."

"Yes, I've seen some things from other worlds in Miami Beach."

"It must've been my family."

———

Some kids enjoy other delusions, the happiest of which is the tooth fairy, that bartering beauty who somehow got into the business of recycling enamel. Kids aren't interested in being touched by an angel, but they love to put the bite on the tooth fairy.

"Who is the tooth fairy?" I asked one lady of eight.

"When your tooth falls out, you put it under your pillow," she replied, "and then the tooth fairy comes at night while you're sleeping and leaves you a quarter."

"And where does she get the quarter?" I said.

"From a rich husband."

This was a perfectly logical answer: A *poor* husband would have had his fairy leave some M&M's or an IOU.

————

Another young lady, one who was six, had a different answer when I said, "Who is the tooth fairy?"

"Well," she said, "that's the fairy that comes and takes the tooth from under your pillow where you put it and leaves money there."

"And what does the tooth fairy do with the tooth?"

"She sells it somewhere."

————

Art received still another view of this sprite from a boy of six.

"How'd you lose all those front teeth?" Art said.

"I left 'em in bubble gum," the boy replied. "I really love bubble gum."

"Even more than your teeth?"

"Yeah."

"And do you do anything with those teeth after you take 'em out of the gum?"

"I put 'em under my pillow and the good fairy brings money."

"And where does she get this money?"

"I think she robs a bank."

How interesting that the boy called this beautiful bandit the good fairy. What would the bad fairy be? One who invaded principal?

———

And so, here we have three different views of the unknown. Is the tooth fairy on an endless allowance from a rich husband who is happy to have her out of the house? Is she an SIF, a single invisible female, who stays in business by selling her collections to people who can't get elephant tusks? Or does her photograph grace the post office?

———

These are the questions that Art and I have grappled with, questions even more profound than "Will Social Security go under?" and "Where did I leave my glasses?" Art, in fact, revealed new dental depths during a trip away from his show, on a day when he took one of his own daughters to an orthodontist.

"Is there anything you'd rather be doing today than going to the orthodontist?" he asked her.

"I'd rather be living in a country where they let the kids' teeth rot," she blithely replied.

She had gotten to the heart of the matter, something

kids do even better than the folks from the IRS. Like all kids, and unlike all adults under eighty, she had boldly said exactly what she was thinking, a style guaranteed to enable a candidate to make a concession speech. No inhibitions form inside a child's mind until about the age of ten, when he or she begins the education that produces a mature and diplomatic liar.

———

In spite of their knowledge that all adults are pathetic liars, kids still seem to want to move up to adulthood themselves, perhaps because they like the challenge of being less ridiculous than the current group. Art and I have asked thousands of kids what they wanted to be when they grew up—that is, something besides the tooth fairy's husband or fence.

"What do you think you want to be when you grow up?" Art asked one boy of six named Drew.

"A bus driver or a pilot," Drew replied.

"Okay, suppose you're flying a plane and all four engines suddenly stop. What would you say?"

" 'Our Father, Who art in heaven . . .' "

To Drew, this response was official FAA procedure.

———

To a girl of seven named Eve-Lynn, Art said, "When you grow up, what do you want to be?"

"A movie star," she replied.

"What does a movie star do?"

"She eats breakfast with other movie stars and eats lunch with other movie stars and she eats dinner with other movie stars and then goes to bed with other movie stars."

That seemed like a pretty good life, certainly a nutritious one, although Art did wonder if the star managed to make any films between her snacks and group sex. He decided, however, to end the interview there, perhaps because he knew less about that particular pajama party than the young lady did.

––––––––

Kids ponder things never pondered at the Institute for Advanced Studies. For example, Art asked one boy of five, "If you were president, what would you do?"

"I'd sit on the pot and think about it," the boy replied.

How many presidents have led the country astray because they did their thinking while wearing their pants?

––––––––

KIDS SAY THE DARNDEST THINGS

Kids have done their deepest thinking about the American economy and have decided that it is better to be rich than poor.

"What do you want to be when you grow up?" I asked a boy named Loren, who was eight.

"A surgeon," he replied.

"And what does a surgeon do?" I said.

"He cuts people up."

"What kind of people?"

"Rich people," he said. "I'll cut rich people up."

Yes, I'm afraid that poor people simply have to learn to stay in one piece.

———

Kids like Loren—and they're *all* like Loren—think about money as creatively as they think about Jesus and the tooth fairy. To one girl of ten, Art said, "What would you do if you woke up one day and found that you were a millionaire?"

"I'd invest the money," she said.

"In what?"

"In stocks."

"Any particular stocks?" said Art, not above getting a tip from a child.

"Yes, IBM and TNT."

I don't know about IBM, but TNT is certainly bound to go up.

———

Art and I both have discovered that kids on TV rarely "go up," the words actors use for losing their poise before an audience.

"Do you like being on TV?" I said to one girl of six.

"I never been on," she replied.

"You're on right now."

"What show is *this*?"

The Twilight Zone.

———

For twenty-three years on *House Party,* Art also received the creative candor that comes only from people whose ages are in single digits.

On one particular show, he was discussing the holidays with a girl of eight.

"You have a little brother?" Art said.

"Yes, I guess so," she replied, unable to fully accept that awful truth.

"And what are you going to give your little brother for Christmas?"

"I haven't decided yet."

"Well, what did you give him last Christmas?"

"Roseola."

———

Kids have warm feelings about their relationships with all members of their families.

"What does your father do for fun?" said Art to a boy of seven.

"He drinks beer and smokes cigars," the boy replied.

"And what does your mother do for fun?"

"She doesn't have any fun."

Art decided not to ask if the woman was a Puritan or a masochist. Perhaps the boy felt that beer and cigars wouldn't do it for Mom and what else *was* there to entertain an adult? He was still too young to have been aware of a pleasant alternate entertainment, but the boy to whom Art spoke next knew there was something more than beer and cigars.

"How did your mother and father meet?" he asked this boy.

"They met at a nudist camp," the boy replied. "They took their clothes off and fell in love."

These two activities usually happen in reverse order, of course: Very few people fall in love *because* they see what's

under the clothes; but whatever the order happens to be, children do not view romance as any part of their parents' marriage.

"What does your mother do?" I asked a girl of six named Laurie.

"She's in charge of everything," Laurie said.

"And what does your father do?"

"I can't remember."

"Isn't he in charge of anything?"

"I'll have to ask my mother."

"Why not ask *him*?"

"Oh, *he* wouldn't know."

———

Children learn early what I learned considerably later in life: I am not the boss of my house. I have seen the boss's job and I don't want it.

"When you get into trouble," I said to Calvin, who was seven, "would you rather deal with your mother or your father?"

"My father," he replied, "because fathers, they're not *real* parents."

———

Of a boy of five, I also asked, "Who's the boss in your family?"

"My dad," he said.

"Really?" I said, feeling like an anthropologist who had made a rare find: The only home in America where the father was the boss, probably because the mother was spending a year on a space station. "Your *father* is the boss?"

"Yeah. If I want to go somewhere, I ask my father and he says 'Yes.' And I can go if my mom lets me."

———

Parents may be confused about the running of the American home, but every kid knows who is captain and who is first mate. Actually, the woman is both captain *and* first mate and her husband is second mate, though sometimes less.

"What does your mother do?" I asked one six-year-old boy.

"She bosses people around," he said.

"Why does she do that?"

"Because people don't know what to do."

"Well, don't *you* know what to do?"

"Not me, *people*. They go bonkers at sleepover parties."

"Isn't that what you're supposed to do at sleepover parties?"

"Not my mother's."

"Remind me not to come."

"You're not invited."

———

In spite of the Equal Rights Amendment, children know that there are more differences between their fathers and their mothers than merely that their mothers don't have any fun.

"What does your father do?" I asked a boy of seven on one of the shows.

"He's an anes . . . anes . . . anester . . ." he crisply replied.

"Anesthesiologist?"

"Yeah, that."

"And what does your mother do?"

"She's a nurse."

"What's the difference?"

"They're not spelled the same way."

The boy, of course, was right: The primary difference between an anesthesiologist and a nurse is that they are *not* spelled the same way. They also are not spelled like chirop-

odist or bigamist. I have never met an adult who pointed this out.

———————

On one of his *House Party* shows, Art discussed nursing with a four-year-old who could spell almost nothing.

"When you grow up," Art asked her, "what do *you* want to be?"

"A nurse," she replied.

"Why do you want to be a nurse?"

"Because they give shots."

"Where?"

"In the room."

And the room can be a tender spot.

———————

Just as I have never met an adult who pointed out that other professions are spelled differently from "nurse," I also have never met an adult who was able to define "grandmother" in just two words.

"What are grandmothers?" I asked a girl of seven.

"Retired mothers," she replied.

"But retired mothers *could* be mothers who've decided to get out of some strenuous profession—like wrestling," I

said. "*You* know: Quit the pro tour, stay home, and flip people *there*."

"Oh, I don't know about *that*," she said.

And I certainly didn't know either. I just knew that talking to a child was playing conversational lottery. The odds against winning were dismaying.

For example, in talking to another young lady, one who was six, I stayed on one sentence too long.

"When you get married, how many children would you like to have?" I asked her.

"One or two," she said.

"Well, that's very nice, but suppose your husband wants twelve?"

"I'll get rid of him."

Right: Let him find a dozen eggs somewhere else.

Children do not understand adults—most adults don't either—because adult social intercourse is not an ideal model for small people.

"Do you like to listen to grown-up talk?" Art asked one boy of five.

"Yes," he said.

"And what kind of things do they say?"

"Shut up."

Of course, "Shut up" was some of the sweeter talk in my old neighborhood, the Philadelphia projects where I spent my boyhood listening to adults as little as I could. The amazing thing about kids is the selectivity with which they listen to adults. They tune out ninety-eight percent, everything from "Brush your teeth" to "No getting married on school nights," but absorb "Shut up," "Go to hell," and certain hand signs that Helen Keller never used.

I didn't really have to listen to my parents because my answer to everything they said was pretty predictable: the handy, all-purpose "No problem." If my mother asked about a note from school wondering why I seemed to be a part-time student, I would blithely reply, "No problem." If my father asked why the dog was painted blue, I would reassuringly reply, "No problem." And if either one of them had said that the district attorney had just secured an indictment against me, I would have cheerfully replied, "No problem."

"Just tell me why the police are after you," said my mother one day.

What a lucky guess.

"Mom, what makes you think somethin' like that?" I said.

"Then what are you doin' home so early?"

"I got tired of foolin' around."

"Bill, if you keep lyin' to me, I'm not comin' to your trial."

"Mom, I tell you: No problem. There's nothin' wrong."

"I had children, that's what's wrong. Okay, go to your room an' think about what Jesus said about lyin' to your mother."

"He was against it, right?"

———

My mother was an optimist: She thought that she could influence her children. However, as Art and I have learned, every once in a while parents do accidentally teach something to their children.

"What's the best time for your parents?" I asked one boy of eight.

"After martinis," he replied.

To this boy, that's the meaning of A.M.

"Well, after martinis, is there anything special that they like to do for fun?"

"I'm trying to find out," he said. "They always lock the door."

KIDS SAY THE DARNDEST THINGS

———

Kids relate to pets better than they relate to people. A pet understands when you say "No problem."

On one of my shows, I asked a girl of six named Linda, "Do you like pets?"

"Oh, yes," Linda replied.

"And do you have any?"

"My only pet is my little brother."

Now, here's the anthropological question: When Linda calls her little brother a "pet," does she mean that he is:

A) something endearing, or

B) an animal.

———

In matters of mammalian gender, kids have charmingly offbeat ideas.

To a boy of eight, Art Linkletter said, "Do you have any pets?"

"Yes," said the boy. "Two dogs."

"What kind are they?"

"One's a boy and one's a fixed girl."

She would have to adopt.

———

On one show, Art got some information that Darwin had missed when he asked a girl of five, "Do you have any pets?"

"Yes," she said, "two dogs."

"Do they have pedigrees?"

"Yes, but not on purpose."

An accidental pedigree is the rarest kind: for example, a dog that becomes a Doberman by mistake.

––––––––

American children possess so much knowledge that I can understand their desire to drastically reduce their time in school.

"If you were president, what would you do?" said Art to a girl of eight.

"I'd change the law so there was only school from nine to ten in the morning," she replied.

"That long, eh?"

"That's enough school."

"What about recess? That used to be my favorite subject."

"Well, you wouldn't go *all* the way from nine to ten. You'd have to have recess too."

"And lunch?"

"Oh, sure, lunch."

"So you'd really be going for about twenty minutes."

"That's fine with *me.*"

Her whole school system would be geared to short attention spans; but a lot of money would be saved by reducing the salaries of teachers, who then could handle their classes in a kind of scholastic drive-through.

———

Kids have always felt that they need neither school nor parents; and having money is optional too.

To a girl of five named Susie, Art said, "If you got lost without money, what would you do?"

"I'd write a check," Susie replied, knowing that it wouldn't clear for at least two days, willing to pay the overdraft fee, and wondering if she had lent her Visa card to Barbie.

———

Kids are as foggy about finances as the Clinton administration has been.

To a boy of six named Paul, I once said, "What does your father do?"

"He's a banker," Paul replied. "He banged into a parked car one time."

"Was he trying to collect on a loan?"

"No, he's not alone. He's in a whole bank full of bankers."

"Does he do anything special in the bank?"

"He does money there."

"You mean he *prints* it?"

"I think so. I'll ask him."

"And ask him if he envisions any change in the prime."

————

Some kids are clearly aware of what their parents do, but some have to guess, just as my mother used to guess what *I* was doing when I was trying to get started in stand-up comedy.

"Can't you do somethin' *legitimate*?" she once said, as if addressing a confidence man. But let's get back to other kids besides me and their mistiness about the world of work.

"Your mother is a doctor?" I said to one woman of five named Nancy.

"That's right," she replied.

"And what is she a doctor *of*?"

"People."

"So she's not a veterinarian."

"What's that?"

"A doctor of animals."

"I don't think any of her patients is animals."

"So what *kind* of doctor is she?"

"A good kind."

"Yes, but is she a good kind with a *specialty*? I mean, does she treat eyes or noses or stomachs or feet?"

"Sick people," said Nancy.

I pressed no further. I certainly had to respect a doctor who specialized in treating the sick.

———

On one *House Party* show, Art had a talk with a girl of six whose dream man might have come from either side of the bars in a zoo.

"What do you want to be when you grow up?" Art asked her.

"A veterinarian or a stewardess," she replied.

"Any particular reason for choosing those two?"

"Because I like animals and men."

In that order? For some reason, Art didn't ask her. He did, however, hope that someday she would be lucky enough to find both in one. Her dream man was the missing link.

In the next chapter, you will taste the fruits of the anthropological exploration that Art and I have done to learn the effect on America's youngest females of the higher mammals in the lower grades.

3.

The Birds and the
Beeswax

.

W hen the kids on Art's show and mine have re-
vealed confusion about sex, I have understood,
because I was the same way as a kid, even a kid of thirty-
six. Kids today, however, are infinitely smarter about the
most popular mechanics than I was in my boyhood days.
The sexual briefing I got from my father avoided textbook
jargon and came directly to the point: One day when I was
twelve, he solemnly took me aside and told me that I was
never to use the men's room in the subway.

This dissertation did leave a certain gap in the story of
reproduction, but I was lucky enough to have learned
friends who filled it in.

"It's somethin' your mother an' father do to each other,"
said Junior Barnes, carefully choosing his words. "Your

mother an' father, they're definitely the ones involved. Y' see . . . well, y' see . . . Cos, this is gonna *kill* ya, 'cause believe me, it's really *stupid.*"

The following generations of kids have also felt that sex involved a certain stupidity, even though it's a stupidity they understand much earlier than twelve.

No matter how sophisticated kids are today in their post-toddler maturity, they still know that sex is fundamentally as mysterious as the schedule of the Long Island Rail Road.

In one memorable moment, Art asked a girl of six, "Melissa, what would make a perfect husband for you?"

And Melissa replied, "A man who could give me a lot of money and loves horses and lets me have twenty-four kids."

"And what do you want to be when you grow up?"

"A nun."

As Rodgers and Hammerstein *should* have written: How do you solve a problem like *Melissa*?

Either light or darkness was shed on the subject a few weeks later, when Art talked to a nine-year-old girl who amended Masters and Johnson by saying, "As for birth

control, I am against it for humans but for it against insects."

Keats couldn't have put it better in a sonnet on Lyme disease.

———————

When she was eight, my own youngest daughter tried to enlighten me about the sexual revolution that I was still confusing with the Russian. As she walked past me in our house one day, she was singing, "Give it to me all night long. Give it to me all night long."

"Give you *what* all night long?" I said, not sure I wanted the answer; in fact, I was sure I *didn't* want the answer.

"I don't know," she told me.

"Then why do you want it all night long?"

"Because it feels so good."

———————

The mystique of human sexuality is nicely illuminated by my daughter's hymn to nothing in particular and by Melissa's remarkable plan to have two dozen undercover deliveries in an abbey. Kids today know that Viagra isn't the capital of Peru, but there are still some things that Art and I can teach them. I've asked Art if he happens to know any.

———

Art, however, is still trying to figure out something a young lady said to him thirty-three years ago.

"How did your mother and father meet?" he asked her.

"Well," she said, "they were running around in a car and they fell in love and got married and two weeks later they had me."

Art is now leaning toward an explanation that involves in Volvo fertilization. Nevertheless, two *weeks* . . . That girl's mother was running around in that car and falling in love and getting married and she *still* was able to time her contractions.

———

Speaking of deliveries, I happened to discuss maternity with one biology major of eight and received a memorable new insight into the magical moment.

"Do you know what it's like having a baby?" I asked her.

"Yeah," she said. "When you're having a baby, you're sitting in a hospital bed yelling, 'Get this kid *out* of me!'"

Have there ever been more winged words to capture the sacred moment of new motherhood? Any woman who

doesn't think, *Get this kid* out *of me!* just isn't paying attention.

———

When discussing sex, many kids seem determined never to be involved in a maternity ward: They are budding celibates, eager to join Melissa in that abbey—except the boys, of course, who'd rather go to a monastery with GameBoy.

"What has your mother told you about men?" I asked one girl of seven.

"They're dogs," she sweetly replied.

At least they're loyal.

———

"What do you think about kissing?" I asked a boy of six named Rick.

"It's really gross," said Rick. "It's a gross thing Mommy and Daddy do."

No doubt it was hardly the only gross thing that his mommy and daddy did, especially if you saw the gross they declared on their tax returns, but it was enough to make Rick go platonic.

"I wonder who invented kissing," I asked him.

"Gross," he said.

"Mr. Gross?"

"Naw."

"*Mrs.* Gross?" I said brightly.

"Yeah, *her*. Only a *girl* could invent something so disgusting!"

The war between men and women has many eager young recruits.

"What's your idea of the perfect girl?" said Art to a boy of eight.

"There aren't any," the boy replied.

And on the same show, to a boy of six, Art said, "What's your idea of the perfect girl?"

"One that don't bother me," he said.

"How do they bother you?"

"They're always chasing me."

"Well, you're a good-looking guy."

"Don't I know it."

"But maybe you don't know something else: Boys are supposed to chase *girls.*"

"Where'd you hear *that*?"

"Oh, it's an old rule."

"Not in *my* house. My father don't chase my mother an' the only thing that chases my sister is dogs."

————

Other boys and girls are also unaware of this ancient rule of pursuit, the rule that says: A man chases a woman until she catches him.

To one girl of ten, I said, "In all your ten years, what's the nicest thing a boy has ever done for you?"

"He moved," she replied, and I heard violins.

————

To another young romantic, a boy of eight named Stanley, I said, "Could you ever see yourself kissing a girl?"

"No!" he said.

"Holding a girl's hand and saying, 'I'll love you forever. I can't *live* without you'?"

"No! No!"

"And if a girl ever said that to *you*, what would you say?"

"I'd say, 'Get out of my face!' "

From the Jerome Kern song with that lilting title.

————

However, a boy of ten on the same show had presented himself to a legion of faces, only some of which had asked him to leave.

"Do you have any girlfriends?" I asked him.

"Yeah, about fifteen," he said.

"It's lonely for you, eh? You really have fifteen girl-friends?"

"I think. Yeah, that's about right."

"I'll bet on your report card it says, 'Plays well with others.'"

"No, it doesn't."

"Well, you're an impressive young man. I mean, you *really* like girls."

"Not that much, but you gotta have one."

"Same for adults."

"I used to have more, but some of 'em dumped me."

"In that crowd, how could you tell? So what is it about you that makes women want you?"

"My ears. They're big."

"Yes, so were Clark Gable's."

"And I can wiggle 'em."

Just imagine the appeal that Clark Gable would have had if he had thought of not merely presenting those ears but activating them too.

KIDS SAY THE DARNDEST THINGS

You see, even the dimmest boy knows that there is something about girls that is definitely different. This knowledge is possessed even by a boy I just heard about. At the start of the term, his fifth-grade teacher had asked the class to fill out cards with home addresses, phone numbers, and an emergency number in case there was a problem at school, such as the school's inability to stand the boy another five minutes.

The boy wrote that his emergency number was 911.

Yes, even *that* boy knows there is something about girls that just doesn't add up. On the other hand, girls know there's something about boys that goes far beyond defective arithmetic. In fact, it is a matter for the Centers for Disease Control.

"Tell me, exactly what's *wrong* with boys?" I asked my youngest daughter one day.

"Daddy, don't you *know*?" she replied.

"Well, I keep meaning to ask your mother . . ."

"Boys have *boy* germs."

"Of course. Pasteur discovered that. But don't girls have *girl* germs?"

"You just don't understand, do you?"

"I guess I don't. The most I can understand is boy Germans. But they keep themselves pretty clean."

———

To satisfy my daughter, I have been digging deeper into the science of why boys and girls are distinctively weird.

"What's the difference between a boy and a girl?" I asked one girl of eight on the show. "I mean, a girl is a boy who can have babies, right?"

"It's their *chromosomes*," she replied, using a word that I hadn't heard until college, when I'd thought it meant color wheels. "My dad taught me about them. The chromosomes tell the body if it should do boy things or girl things."

"You mean if it should go to war or lose its sense of direction."

"You see, the boy is XY and the girl is XX. Like 'The X-Files.' "

———

The little I *have* learned about sex is that the Y chromosome in the male is what enables him to live in that great fog bank called his mind; and women know this.

"Have you ever been in love?" I said to a female who was eight.

"Yes," she replied.

"You're only eight. At what age were you in love?"

"Seven."

"But you're not seeing him anymore?"

"No."

"Is that because he hasn't had all his shots?"

"No, he was cute, but he wasn't very smart."

Of course: He was a boy; and, as that sophisticated woman of six once told me, "*You* know how *boys* are: stupid." We men should have tried to keep our shortage of brain cells a secret—certainly from *women.* Somehow we have to find a way to be smarter. Just look how we keep behaving:

"What's a summer romance?" I asked one boy of six.

"When you go out and meet a girl and if you're lucky enough you get engaged," he replied.

"That happens in the summer?"

"Right."

"And what happens in the winter?"

"You dump her."

Now, I suspect that women have gotten tired of the dumpers and have decided that we should concentrate on garbage instead. I really can't blame them, for our intellect—if that's what we're allowed to call it—needs serious work.

"In what other period would you like to have lived?" I asked a boy of nine named Dennis.

"In the Stone Age," Dennis replied.

"Why?"

"Because a man made his wife do all the work."

"And what if she didn't?"

"He went after her with a club."

Dennis didn't know it, but he was already *in* the Stone Age.

Girls, of course, are aware of the primitive nature of their opposites.

"When do you think a girl becomes mature?" I asked a young lady of eight.

"When the boys start slugging you," she said.

"And are *you* mature?"

"Since the first grade."

And so, the challenging mission of a young American woman is to find a man who doesn't behave like one.

"What kind of man would make a good husband?" I asked a girl of eight.

"I'm not sure," she replied. "I just don't want to get stuck with a bum."

Didn't Snow White say the same thing?

By the time they are six, kids know that boys and girls are members of different species. A boy thinks that a girl is deeply flawed, but he's not smart enough to figure out how; and a girl knows that a boy has a brain that simply stopped evolving when there was still a long way to go. The wisdom of the female can reach an awesome level.

For example, Art asked a girl of nine, "What do you have to find out about a man before marrying him?"

"His address," she replied.

Because girls possess such wisdom, boys are often uneasy.

"How old are you, Henry?" said Art to one young man.

"Ten and three-quarters," Henry replied.

"What's your philosophy of life?"

"I'm high about life but low about girls."

"For any particular reason?"

"I have a dim look of them."

Knowing that Henry wasn't talking about cataracts, Art said, "Well, is there something special about girls that you don't like?"

"No," said Henry, "it's nothing special. It's *everything*. I'm really glad I'm not one of 'em."

"You mean it's better to be a boy."

"It's better to be a horse."

"Henry, when you grow up, what do you want to be?"

"I want to follow in my dad's footsteps."

"What is he?"

"I don't know."

———

It is one of the more amusing parts of the human comedy: While adults are acting with nervous sexual correctness, afraid to even shake hands too warmly, the kids are routinely enjoying hand-to-hand combat, the boys using their greater physical strength to make themselves losers to the smarter girls. If boys understood things just a little better, they would still be clueless. To wit—and that's a word that applies to only *one* sex:

"Do you know how your mother and father met?" I asked one boy of eight.

"Well, they were fooling around at work and then they got me," he replied.

Was this a woman who had topped even that two-week gestation period? Kids clearly have no attention span for gestation.

———

And their view of birth is not always one that you would hear from an obstetrician.

"Do you know how a baby is born?" I asked Monroe, who was six.

"Yeah," he said. "The baby falls down and the mother catches it."

Yes, of course, but only if she happens to be a short-stop—and a *good* one: Catching a baby on the short hop is the toughest play in maternity.

———

A girl a year younger than Monroe also had a grasp of obstetrics that wasn't particularly profound.

"What does the stork do?" I asked her.

"He brings the baby to the mommy," she said.

"But where does the stork *get* the baby to bring to the mommy?"

"At the baby place."

"And where is *that*?"

"I think it's at the mall."

———

Art Linkletter's *House Party* kids may have thought that the stork brought babies from some distant field, but many of today's kids are sophisticated enough to realize that the stork brings its babies from the uterus. Armed with this knowledge, today's kids have accepted the grim thought that eventually they will have to be involved with their opposites.

"What is love?" said Art to one girl of seven.

"When you're at school," she said, "and someone chases you."

"But suppose you're being chased just for fun."

"Oh, that's love, not fun."

"But don't you get chased by *lots* of different boys?"

"Yeah, all the ones that love me."

"About how many, would you say?"

"I never stopped to count 'em, but *lots*."

"Is that the best thing about school?"

"Well, lunch is good too."

———

Physical pursuit seems to be central to the kids who play the mating game, as I learned from one girl who was six.

"Do you like boys?" I asked her.

"One of 'em," she replied.

"So he's your special guy."

"No, we're going to get married."

"Don't you think you should check out some other guys?"

"No, one's all I need."

"But it still might be a good idea to look around some more. You know, some girls keep looking till they're almost nine or ten before they decide to get married."

"No, he's the one."

"Why do you like him so much?"

" 'Cause he chases me a lot."

"And you let him catch you?"

"Of course. Your husband's *gotta* catch you."

———

And so, for the women of the newest generations, the most important thing in school is romantic ring-a-lievio; and the ideal husband is not a brain surgeon or a man with a chain of garages: He is a fetching point guard with speedy moves to the basket. And for the boys who do the chasing, the key is to get down as many bets as they can.

"You have a girlfriend?" I asked one boy of eight.

"I got a lot of 'em," he said.

"Why a lot?"

" 'Cause some of 'em might dump me."

"Can you *blame* them for dumping you if they have to share you with so many others?"

"But they don't *know* that."

"Well, if you have so many women," I said to this harem director, "it can't hurt when one of them dumps you."

"Well, I don't like to be dumped. A man's gotta be the Dumpster."

"You mean the *dumper.*"

"Yeah, the guy that throws the woman out."

"But, you know, women don't *like* to be dumped."

"Who told you that?"

"Women. Who told *you* that a man's gotta be the dumper?"

"I heard it on TV."

Here was a young man who badly needed to switch to *Sesame Street.*

———

Although highly intelligent men with a deep understanding of the potential for stupidity that boys have, Art and I have never been able to keep them from realizing that potential

in impressive ways. I did, however, give a brief course in mathematics to one boy of seven after I had asked him, "How would you describe the perfect wife?"

"Twenty-four, thirty-six, twenty-four," he replied, describing either a woman who looked like an egg or the IQs of the Three Stooges.

"I think you mean thirty-six, twenty-four, thirty-six," I said.

"What's the difference?"

"Nothing, if you don't mind your dream girl resembling Humpty Dumpty."

———

Art and I also have come to terms with the dismaying fact that women do not dream of us, or think of us when they're awake.

"Who are the five best-looking men in the world?" I asked one girl of seven.

"My father is number one," she said, aware that *I* wasn't going to pay her college tuition.

"A wise choice," I said. "But what men on the list aren't relatives?"

"Well, Denzel Washington is second . . . Tom Cruise third . . . Brad Pitt fourth . . . and . . ."

"Anyone you happen to be talking to right now?"

"Okay . . . you."

"What a lovely thought. And do you hope to get married one day?"

"Yes, but I'll have to dump him."

"That's not what your mother would do."

"But I have to move on to *Denzel.*"

Yes, some of the kids have been ready for romance, but Art and I kept finding others who felt that the birds and the bees were involved in a dumb design.

"You're a handsome fellow," I told a boy of eight named Dwayne.

"That's right," said Dwayne, who was an agreeable fellow too.

"Did you ever kiss a girl?"

"No," he said, "and I never *will*! That's *disgusting*!"

"I've heard that before."

"Not from me, but I'm tellin' ya: No kissing."

"Well, would you do *anything* with a girl?"

"What kind of girl?"

"The human kind."

"No, not that kind."

"Do you *know* any girls?"

"There's too many of 'em at school."

"Yes, they let them go these days."

"And they keep raisin' their hands."

"Because they know the answers," I said.

But Dwayne knew the most important answer of all, one that should have been posted on a sign at school that had a diagonal red slash through a drawing of his lips: NO KISSING.

———

On another show, a boy who was six eloquently confirmed Dwayne's heartfelt view of American women.

"If a man is in love with a woman," I asked him, "what should he do?"

"Do something different," the boy replied.

What inspirational wisdom! Since everything is different from love, if you subscribe to this philosophy instead of to *Field and Stream,* then love becomes your springboard to playing squash or getting a haircut or reading *A Boy's Life of Fats Domino.*

———

Most boys know the basic truths about women: They are a lower form full of germs that should never be kissed or loved or allowed into polite society. However, a few boys have given the matter even more thought.

"What makes a girl charming?" said Art Linkletter to a boy of nine.

"Her figure and her body," he replied.

"*Both* of those things."

"Yeah."

"What about the way she speaks?"

"She doesn't have to speak."

"You mean you don't want her to speak?"

"No, she can speak if she wants to."

"Don't you think a girl's voice is pretty?"

"If you listen, I guess."

And there you have it: the Young American Male, valiantly trying to reverse the entire Age of Feminism.

———————

As they approach puberty, today at about seven or eight, boys do manage to transcend their feelings about girls to accept the fact that some of them will have to become wives.

"How do you find a wife?" I asked one boy of eight.

"Well, if you don't have a wife," he said, "you hook up with one."

"You know how to do that?"

"Oh, yeah, I'm a good hooker-upper."

"Could you hook *me* up?"

"What kind of wife you want?"

"Oh . . . a woman about sixty, who's thirty-six, twenty-four, thirty-six."

"I don't understand. Which one you want? A woman who's sixty or thirty-six?"

"Well, all right, I'll take one who's thirty-six."

"You don't want those other three?"

"No, thirty-six is my dream girl. And I want her to be . . . to be . . . a former Miss Universe."

"Miss what?"

"Universe."

"Where's that?"

"Near Tennessee."

"Sure, I can hook you up."

And he'd better do it before they hook me up to something else.

————

I probably should have told that boy that I've been happily hooked up for many years to a woman who *is* my universe. However, like Art, I can never resist the exploration of a child's mind, a territory for which nobody has ever had a map.

In exploring kids' thoughts about gender differences, Art took one particular safari that reached an awesome dead end.

"Do you have any brothers or sisters?" he asked a young woman of four named Katie.

"I think I have two brothers," Katie replied.

"You *think*?" said Art. "Haven't you counted them?"

"Yes, two."

"And what are their names?"

"I think one is Sandra."

"Sandra? Isn't that a girl's name?"

"I guess that isn't his name."

"Or else she isn't your brother. What's your other brother's name?"

"I don't know. He never told me."

Before you start wondering about this child, ask yourself: Did *your* brother ever bother to introduce himself to you? Maybe *he* was named Sandra.

————

Kids have their own unique logic; and the only adults who might be able to understand it are the ones in the CIA, who have shown an impressive talent for being unable to foresee every major world event since the collapse of the Soviet Union. A CIA agent would understand something not spo-

ken but written by a child, whose teacher shared it with
Art:

*Though I am now a child, I will one day be a man or a
woman.*

Doesn't that say it all about our changing world?

4.

And Columbus Discovered Columbus Circle

Kids love history; and as every married adult knows, it is possible to love something you don't understand.

"How far back can you remember?" I asked one girl of eight.

"Nothing," she replied.

Of course, she had an excuse: She hadn't been studying the scene for too long. However, *adults* don't know any history either, so kids couldn't know less. Well, some of them *do* know less, but this is what they have to know less than:

Last June 6, I said to a man in his twenties, "You know, today is the anniversary of D day."

"When were A, B, and C?" he replied.

"No, it was the invasion of France."

"What did we have against France?"

Other kids know just as much about World War II as that young man.

"What do you know about World War Two?" Art once asked a boy who was ten.

"Oh, I know a lot," he replied. "World War Two was fought all over the world and other places."

"And do you know the countries that fought?" said Art, eager to plumb the depths of this semi-scholar.

"Sure. America and Great Britain."

"Right! Against whom did they fight?"

"Each other. That's how we got our freedom."

"Yes, I see. Sometimes they also call that the American Revolution."

"Whatever."

"Well, as long as we're talking about that, do you happen to know the cause of the American Revolution?"

"Yeah. No taxation without recreation."

Kids not only understand the principle of no taxation without recreation, a principle stirringly sounded when

Patrick Henry said, "Give me liberty or give me debt," they also understand the workings of American government today.

"Do you know how many United States senators come from each state?" said Art to a girl of nine.

"Oh, yes," she replied. "Each state elects two centaurs."

————

Many kids are just as knowledgeable as those.

"I hear you're good at history," said Art, a man who just won't learn, to a boy of ten.

"Oh, yes," the boy proudly replied.

"Well, do you happen to know when the Magna Carta was signed?"

"At twelve o'clock," he said.

Can we say he is wrong? Of course, noon at the Magna Carta was four A.M. in Los Angeles, but I presume the boy gave local time.

————

Time is what kids can see with such freewheeling fancy. Einstein said that time was curved, but a kid can turn it into a pretzel, as this boy of seven did:

"Who was Elvis Presley?" I asked him.

"He was dead," the boy replied.

If you corrected the boy by saying "Elvis is *still* dead," would that make his answer wrong?

———

Kids simply find meanings and connections that conventional historians have missed, no matter how loose the connections may be.

For example, Art said to one girl of nine, "Who was Paul Revere?"

"False," the girl replied.

She clearly was taking the third-grade pass-fail. Had I heard her answer, I would have said, "No, Paul Revere was *true. Benedict Arnold* was false."

———

In dealing with history, often from the bottom of the deck, kids don't memorize dates because they know that history should be more than a collection of dates—or maybe less. There is, however, one special date that I feel every child should know; and on one particular show, I tried to draw it from a child named Eve, who was nine.

"Eve," I said, "do you know who was born in Philadelphia on July 12, 1937?"

116

"Somebody," she replied, reminding me of how I used to answer exam questions at college after somehow forgetting to read the book.

"Yes, of course," I said. "There always seems to be somebody being born, especially in Philadelphia. But this was somebody *great.*"

"Abraham Lincoln?"

"No, he wasn't lucky enough to be born in Philadelphia. I'm thinking of someone *else* who should be on Mount Rushmore, someone who has many of Lincoln's qualities."

"Leonardo DiCaprio?"

"No, Eve, *I* was born in Philadelphia on July 12, 1937."

"You were? Did you know any old history people?"

"No, just an old history teacher."

Did she think I had known the *first* Eve?

The problem may be that there is simply too much old history for a kid to learn. Kids like *new* history that goes back not much further than the previous week.

———

A boy named Arthur explained this problem to me one day, telling me more than I wanted to know.

"Tell me, Arthur," I made the mistake of saying, "how would you change history?"

"I would leave out that part that's taught in school," he replied.

"Then I'm afraid that not much would have happened."

"That's okay. Too much stuff happened anyway."

———————

The pleasure in having an intellectual exchange with a kid is you never know what surprising new fact you will learn, even if it's not true.

"Do you know anything about the Panama Canal?" I asked one boy, who was nine.

"Sure," he said, "what do you want to know?"

"Well, who built it?"

"Donald Trump?"

"No, I think Donald built the Suez. I mean, what *country* built the Panama Canal?"

The boy took a few seconds to think, something I keep intending to do myself.

"Well," he said, "you don't really *build* a canal. It's just there."

Only a kid can give you a refreshing new way to look at all the money America wasted digging through Panama.

———————

KIDS SAY THE DARNDEST THINGS

If you think kids know history, and I have no idea why you would, their grasp of geography is equally slippery. What the kids I've met on my show hope to be able to do someday is go deep enough into geography so they can spell it. However, on *House Party,* in the days when schools taught geography instead of self-esteem, the kids that Art met could have taken Stanley to Livingstone.

For some reason, on one of his shows, Art fell into a discussion with a ten-year-old girl about the names of certain Europeans; and suddenly Art realized why his job and mine have been so much better than legitimate work.

"There's a special name for people who live in Paris," said Art. "Do you know what it is?"

"Yes," said the girl. "People who live in Paris are called parasites."

And the folks in Berlin are called germs.

———

Kids come so heartbreakingly close to knowing geography, but then the connection is broken. And the breaks are often delicious.

"Mobile is a city presently located in Alabama," a boy of eight said to Art.

Perhaps he knew something about a fault line.

And perhaps Art found a higher wisdom in a boy of eight when Art asked him, "Do you know why so much of the world is covered with water?"

And the boy replied, "Because so little of it is covered with land."

Can you call that answer wrong? It *is* the shortage of land that is responsible for all the water, a fact that no environmentalist has bothered to address.

Art has never gotten credit for some of the astounding scholarship that he inspired on *House Party* with questions even deeper than "Why did you paint your sister green while she was sleeping?" One stunning revelation came when Art said to a boy of ten, "What is the international date line?"

"The international date line," said the boy, "is where people can go to make dates with those of a foreign sex."

How much of the world's trouble is caused by foreign sex! Let us hope that American kids have the patriotic fervor to keep all their sex domestic.

KIDS SAY THE DARNDEST THINGS

Kids are always happy to share with you whatever they know, no matter how little it is.

"What do you know about taxes?" I asked one boy of nine whose name was Darnell Monroe. The name Monroe might have been a sign that he was connected to history, although he probably wasn't related to James.

"What do you want to know?" Darnell replied.

"Well, who started all this tax stuff?"

"Washington, Lincoln, Clinton . . . nobody knows."

But if we ever *find* the guy, he has a lot to answer for.

Another young scholar, a girl of seven, was equally enlightening when I discussed history with her.

"Do you happen to know what Labor Day is?" I asked her.

"Labor Day is the day when everything is on sale," she said.

Or is it the day when the manager sees his shadow?

All right, kids may have a fact or two wrong; they may think that Labor Day honors maternity, but they sometimes see more clearly than many of us who see neither the forest *nor* the trees.

Art Linkletter, for example, was given a splendid burst of insight when he discussed Thanksgiving with a young woman of six.

"At Thanksgiving, what are you thankful for?" he asked her.

"That I'm an American," she replied.

"That's a fine answer."

"That's right."

"But tell me," said Art, "what *is* an American?"

The young woman paused, for she wanted to give no childish answer to such a momentous question.

"An American," she finally said, "is someone who lives in Los Angeles."

Now, this was good for Art to learn because he had long suspected California of being a foreign country. Art was born in Canada, not the smartest thing for a person to do, and it has taken him a while to learn all the states. I, on the other hand, have always *known* all the states: bewilderment, dizziness, dismay, and disgust, especially when I'm looking for my glasses.

Kids are particularly wise in divining the essence of Colonial times. In fact, I once asked a boy of seven, "What were Colonial times?"

"A newspaper," he replied. "In another state or country."

Actually, he was only half right: *Colonial Times* was bought by *USA Today* the same year that Benjamin Franklin decided that eighty was not too old for chasing women, especially when he looked so dapper.

"How do you think Benjamin Franklin looked?" I asked a girl of nine outside Philadelphia's Independence Hall.

"He wore a suit," she said. "Like someone going to dinner in Atlantic City."

"Did Benjamin Franklin like Atlantic City?"

"He didn't go to Atlantic City much. He liked it in Philadelphia."

"You know, *I* grew up in Philadelphia and sometimes I went to Atlantic City."

"No kidding," she said. "You know any guys from the olden days?"

"You mean like Benjamin Franklin?"

"You couldn't know *him*. I mean some of the *younger* olden guys."

"Like which ones?" I said.

"You know Lincoln?"

"I keep telling you kids: Lincoln wasn't from Philadelphia."

It all runs together in those little heads, and time takes on a new meaning. For example, while gathering new views of history that day at Independence Hall, I left Lincoln and discussed a different contemporary of mine, Betsy Ross, with a girl of eight.

"Do you know who Betsy Ross was?" I asked her.

"Sure," she replied. "She was a supermodel who helped to end slavery."

Her answer rocked me, because it contained two sublimely cockeyed dimensions. However, I soon had a second thought: Since the story of Betsy Ross sewing the first American flag is fiction, who can say for certain that she *didn't* fight against slavery? Or was that Diana Ross?

This is what happens when you start discussing history with kids. Your connections loosen and pretty soon you're wondering if the South Pole was discovered by Admiral Byrd or Larry.

Because those kids at Independence Hall weren't striking me as potential Rhodes scholars, I decided to make my questions easier.

"Do you know what happened in 1492?" I asked a boy of nine.

"Oh, *somethin'* happened," he brightly said.

"Yes, it was that kind of year: Things were happening every day. But I'm thinking of something *special* that happened in 1492 that didn't happen in 1926."

"Fourteen ninety-two . . . fourteen ninety-two . . ."

He was saying it as if expecting a snap from center.

"I'll give you a hint: It was a famous year in American history," I said, now so confused by the kids that I'd forgotten there *was* no American history in 1492.

"The Declaration of Independence was signed?"

"No, they were still working on it, but something special was discovered that year."

I expected him to say "Penicillin."

"Yeah!" he cried. "Frozen yogurt!"

I took world history at Temple and I happen to know that frozen yogurt wasn't discovered till just after the French Revolution, but I didn't want to discourage him. I love the way that kids rewrite history; adults do it less entertainingly.

———

The person who should be teaching history to kids, the person who would best understand them, is Yogi Berra.

Yogi would appreciate the acumen of the boy who told Art, "I don't believe Columbus is as famous as most people think he is," and the girl who gave Art the most sensible explanation of why Peter the Great was called Peter the Great and not Sam Koslovsky.

"His mother named him his first name and he named himself the rest," she said.

———

I'm afraid that boy was wrong: It turns out that Columbus probably *is* as famous as most people think.

"Do you know who discovered America?" I asked a girl named Marcia, who was nine.

"Christopher Columbus," she said.

"Right. And do you know what he *thought* he discovered?"

"What do you mean?"

"I mean, he sailed the wrong way."

"He didn't use the boat right?"

"No, he used the boat right, but he went in the wrong direction."

"How come?"

"Well—and this is interesting if I can remember it—he thought he was discovering some *other* country," I said, wondering why it would need discovering if it was already a

country. Talking to kids can do that to your head, even if it wasn't much to begin with.

"Italy?" said Marcia.

"No, Italy was already discovered by the Italians. Some *other* country."

"France?"

"No, but that's another good guess."

"I give up."

"He thought he had found *India*."

"So why did he come to *America*?"

"I give up too."

———

Art has also done distinguished work in digging up the truth about Columbus. To a boy of nine, he said, "Do you know who *Nina, Pinta,* and *Santa Maria* were?"

"Sure," said the boy. "They were the women who gave Columbus the money for his trip."

Or else they were the women his *sailors* gave money to *before* the trip. At any rate, Columbus wasn't happy to have to leave them on the dock.

———

A person who is almost as famous as most people think he is is Ferdinand Magellan, the Portuguese navigator who

tried to sail around the entire earth to prove that it was round, probably because he didn't think that Columbus should be so famous. Just as I have done groundbreaking scholarship about Columbus with the kids, Art has been equally successful in enriching our knowledge of Magellan, whether or not you want to know anything else about him.

To a girl of nine, Art said, "Can you tell me who Magellan was?"

"Yes," she replied, feeling she had given a complete answer.

After a pause, during which he wondered if it would have been more intellectually fulfilling to host a Miss Universe pageant, Art said, "Well, who *was* he?"

"Magellan made the first trip around the world," she said. "And when he got back, he told how he had been killed in Spain."

No *wonder* he was famous.

For some reason, Art then felt compelled to keep doing public relations for Magellan. On another show, he asked a boy who was eight, "Do you know who Magellan was?"

"Yeah, he was a sailor with Columbus," the boy replied.

"No," said Art, "Magellan booked himself on a later

ship, one that sailed in his lifetime. He was an explorer just as great as Columbus. Haven't you heard of him?"

"Oh, yeah, he was a *different* guy."

"Right! And do you know *why* he explored?"

"Magellan explored because he was curious. A lot of people kept saying, 'Isn't Magellan a curious person?' "

And even more people keep saying, "Aren't Linkletter and Cosby curious people to try to have conversations with kids that contain connections?"

———

In one particular conversation, there was a certain connection that needed an electrician. Deciding to sail away from Magellan, Art asked a boy of eight, "In what channel was the Spanish armada defeated?"

"I think it was Channel Four," the boy said.

Channel Four is just one of the channels where Art and I have been defeated many more times than the Spanish armada.

———

Art and I both like to learn incorrect things about the whole world, but American history is *my* particular field of misinformation. I especially like talking to the kids about

129

those legends of American history: George Washington, Napoleon, and Betsy Ross.

That day at Independence Square, when my own understanding of history grew even dimmer, I kept coming back to Betsy Ross.

"Tell me about Betsy Ross," I said to a boy of seven.

"Well, she lived in Philadelphia," he said.

"Not far from right here, didn't she?"

"Yeah, on Bainbridge, near the 7-Eleven."

"That was *here* then?"

"Yeah, Bainbridge was here. A lot of streets was."

"And what did Betsy Ross make?"

"Some kind of pudding."

"She sewed *pudding*?"

"Yeah, your kind."

"Betsy Ross made *Jell-O*?"

"She *didn't*?"

Maybe she did; for, as Yogi Berra and ten million kids would say, everything that's known about Betsy Ross isn't. There is no proof that she sewed anything more than Jefferson's shorts. She might even have sewn bundles for Britain.

KIDS SAY THE DARNDEST THINGS

The biggest member of my big three—Napoleon was a little guy—was George Washington, whose memory moved a young man of eight to eloquence when I talked to him on the show. His name was Michael and his look was so serious that I instantly knew that he had thought about a lot of things, though not completely.

"Michael," I said, "can you tell me the name of the first president?"

At once, his face shifted into the look of concentration that seizes a child when asked if he has remembered to do any homework this year.

"The first president," said Michael, "was that guy who cheated on his wife. I forget his name."

How lucky for that president that Michael is protecting his identity.

————

A few years before Michael's dramatic revelation about a man who could have been the father of a lot of our country, I gained my own insight into the first president from a child of nine, who happened to be one of my own.

I had been driving through central New Jersey with my wife and two of my daughters, when we came to an old house whose sign informed us that it had been the headquarters of George Washington during the Revolution. A

few minutes later, however, we came to another old house with a sign that said it had been Washington's headquarters.

"How do you like that?" I said to my passengers. *"Another* Washington's headquarters."

And my daughter Erika replied, "It must be a franchise."

———

Kids like to dream about being president; and, unlike many older candidates, they have ideas about the job.

"Would you like to be president of the United States?" said Art Linkletter to one six-year-old boy who was weighing his career choices.

"I couldn't be president," the boy replied. "I don't even know who's fighting."

———

Yes, knowing who's fighting should be a prerequisite for government service, but often it isn't.

A few years ago, as a joke, a reporter asked a few congressmen, "Are you in favor of American aid to Fredonia?"

"Of course," one of them said. "Fredonia is strategically important to us."

And it was strategically even more important to the Marx Brothers.

Had Art or I asked one of the kids "Are you in favor of American aid to Fredonia?" we undoubtedly would have received a more sensible answer, something like: "Why should we help Fredonia? She has girl germs."

————————

"If you became president," I asked one eight-year-old, "what would you do?"

"I'd have to ask my mother," he replied.

"But some presidents do the job without asking their mothers. Suppose she was at the market and you had to run the country by yourself. What would you do?"

"I'd go to bed," he said, "and let the vice president do all the work."

"I'm not sure if the Constitution is clear about naps outside the Cabinet room," I told him, "but if you do nod off on the presidency, who would you like to *be* your vice president?"

"Santa Claus."

"So you're a Democrat."

"What's that?"

"No one really knows."

At eight, the boy already understood Will Rogers's words: "I belong to no organized political party. I'm a Democrat."

At least one of the kids I've met saw the presidency as a role that might be even *too* entertaining for her father.

"Would you like your dad to be president?" I asked a girl who was six.

"Oh, no," she replied. "Because then he'd have to go out and champagne."

It was the champagning, of course, that ruined Harding and Grant.

Kids appreciate the virtue of sober discretion, especially in the Oval Office. To one six-year-old girl, Art said, "If you were president, what's the first thing you would do?"

"Keep my mouth shut," she replied.

This policy might have a certain effect on her inaugural address, but the speeches generally run too long anyway.

Perhaps the richest seminar on history took place when I went one on one with a boy of nine named Donald, who said that history was one of his two favorite subjects.

"What's the other?" I asked him.

"Arm wrestling," he said.

"Yes, I majored in that. And I minored in detention. Okay, so let's talk about history. Do you have any heroes?"

"Yeah, Scottie Pippin."

"Do you by any chance mean Pippin, the king of France?"

"He in the NBA?"

"No, he was drafted for jousting. Well, speaking of heroes, and I'm not sure we were, would you rather be John F. Kennedy or Abraham Lincoln?"

"Don't matter to me. Either way I'm dead."

"I never looked at it that way. I guess our greatest hero of all is George Washington. Do you know much about him?"

"Oh, yeah, plenty. He never told a lie."

"That's right."

"I don't believe it," said Donald. "Did *he* say he never told a lie? 'Cause if he did, that's one right there."

"No, actually it's *people* who've said it."

"Did they *know* 'im? I mean, come *on*. You standin' there and tellin' me the dude never once said . . . *you* know, he was goin' to do United States stuff when he was really goin' for a beer?"

"Now that you put it that way, Donald . . . but look: He did lead our army in winning the American Revolution. And do you know why we needed that revolution?"

"Yeah, King George didn't want us to have our freedom. I don't know why, but it wasn't a very good reason."

"Well, King George was crazy."

"Why'd they let him be king?"

"Well, to be king, you don't need anyone's permission."

"You mean you just *say* it? Like in checkers? 'King me!' That's cool."

"Would you like to be a king?"

"Sure, if other stuff doesn't work out. My father wants me to be a lawyer."

"They do better than kings. The king business is in a slump. You know, they offered George Washington the job of king and he turned it down."

"He *did*? He was crazy too."

"No, he said America fought the Revolution to get rid of the king, so he decided to become president instead. And after he was through being president, you know what he did?"

"Oh, yeah, I know that: He retired to his rusty home in Mount Vernon."

"No, Donald, his *rustic* home."

"That's what I said."

"You said a *rusty* home. That's a home that needs oiling. Do you know anything else about George Washington?"

"No, I wasn't born."

"Believe it or not, neither was I. Donald, who is the person you *most* admire?"

"I don't know."

"Is it *me*?"

"Oh, no, it's not you."

"Yes, the odds were definitely against it. Okay, tell me this: You couldn't meet George Washington, but if you could meet one famous person, who would it be?"

"Not you."

"Yes, you said that. We've already met and I know it's not doing much for you. Speaking of history, Donald, and I'm not so sure we are, you know who my *other* favorite character is?"

"I like Dennis Rodman."

"Yes, Dennis Rodman certainly has a place in history and I'll keep looking for it. But the man I have in mind is Benjamin Franklin."

"I heard of him."

"Even though you weren't born. Well, do you know what Franklin did?"

"He invented lightning. He took a kite, stuck a key on it, and got hit by lightning."

"Yes, quite a science project. Didn't that sting?"

"Oh, it hurted him down to the bone."

"Would you do something like that?"

"No, lightning's already been invented."

I had gone one on one with Donald and he had double-teamed me. This boy was *The* Donald and he had made me feel like Mickey Mouse.

5.

Renaissance Minds: Or Perhaps from the Inquisition

There is no way to contain a kid's breadth of knowledge because it is knowledge enriched by ignorance—in other words, a mind that would feel at home in Congress. On Art's show and mine, we have found the highest expression of this mind and the lowest too; it is often hard to tell them apart. Once kids have finished holding forth on the Bible, their families, sex, and history, their minds tend to spin off in several directions at once.

For example, the insight I gained from one boy of six can be considered to transcend Hindu philosophy. And it also managed to transcend Western sense.

"What's your favorite game?" I asked him.

"Basketball," he replied.

"With whom do you play?"

"Usually nobody."

"You mean you play by yourself."

"Yeah."

"Then you always win."

"Sometimes."

I called Leonard Stern, commissioner of the National Basketball Association, to see if he could figure this out. He put me on hold.

In a similar moment, I once said to a young woman of ten, "If you could meet one famous person, who would it be?"

"Liza Minnelli," the girl replied.

"You know who her mother was?"

"Nancy Reagan."

I didn't push this further because I know that show business people have unusual ways of getting involved with one another.

————

One minute a kid will redefine strangeness; the next minute he or she will give you a breathtaking epiphany, which a kid would say is a famous jewelry store.

For example, to a girl of six I once said, "Do you like broccoli?"

"No," she replied.

"But broccoli is *good* for you."

"Not for *me*. I hate it. I've never eaten it."

"If you've never eaten it, how do you know you hate it?"

"I just know things like that."

———

Yes, at certain times kids know so much more than we do, especially you. To a boy the same age as that girl, I once said, "What do you want to be when you grow up?"

"A pet doctor," he replied.

"Oh, a veterinarian."

"No, a pet doctor."

"That's the same thing."

"So why do they call it different?" he said.

"I'm sorry I brought it up. Okay, pet doctor, here's a question for you. I've got this bird."

"What kind of bird?"

"A parakeet."

"Yeah, they're cute."

"Not *this* one. He's just lying on the bottom of the cage and he's perfectly still and his eyes are closed."

"He's dead."

What diagnosis did I *expect*? That the bird was the picture of health? The bird might have been *lying* on a picture of health if the AMA journal were under him.

———————

I did a better study of domestic zoology when I asked a girl of five named Marjorie about pets, hoping she had one that happened to be alive and that was not a scorpion or crocodile.

"Do you have any pets?" I asked her.

"Well, I *had* a pet skunk," Marjorie replied.

Oh-oh. Another autopsy.

"You don't have him anymore?" I said.

"He died."

"Gosh, I'm sorry. I'm always sorry when a skunk dies." But not one that lives indoors.

"His name was Rosebud," Marjorie said.

"Lovely," I said, wondering if Rosebud's name had fooled anyone into thinking he was a raccoon. "Where is he now?"

"In skunk heaven."

"And what's it like in skunk heaven?"

"Smelly."

Did I expect it to be attar of roses?

———————

Kids' fantasies are often touching and we adults must never dispel them; and so, I didn't tell this nasally challenged

young lady that if God didn't want a dead dog, He certainly didn't want Rosebud, even if Rosebud had been called St. Paul. Adults must let kids nurture their delusions, just as they let us nurture ours by allowing us to think they are paying attention to anything we say.

Another one of my delusions is that I can ask a question that doesn't strike a child as dumb.

"Do you have any pets?" I asked a girl of five.

"Yes," she said, "a goldfish."

"Has it ever died?"

Has it ever died?

After hearing myself ask that question, I wondered if I should return at least part of my salary to CBS. However, kids have no trouble handling such thoughts; and since there is a little kid inside all of us, I encouraged mine to continue making no sense.

"Yes," she said, "every week."

And so, here we had a girl with a goldfish that died once a week, an event that *had* to be bad for the fish. It was time for me to give just a dusting of logic to our dialogue.

"The same fish?"

"No," she said thoughtfully, "I think it's a different one."

"So you replace the dead fish with another one and then you always have a fresh one to die."

"They all look alike anyway."

"A very tender thought. How do you *know* when a fish is dead?"

"They don't move."

"And what do you do with them?"

"I flush them down the toilet."

Good, because God doesn't want *them* either.

––––––––

A few weeks later, to a girl a year older than the sentimental flusher, I said, "Do you have a pet?"

"Yes," she replied, "a dog."

"Does it have a pedigree?"

"Yes."

"Do you know what a pedigree is?"

"No."

"It means the dog is from a fine family."

"It's from a store."

"Which was run by a fine family, I'm sure."

A kid has to get up early in the afternoon to top *me*.

––––––––

Kids have a much deeper understanding of pets than adults do. To one girl of seven, Art said, "Do you have a pet?"

"I once had a dog," she replied, "but he got married and moved to Oakland."

Art is a very bright man, but even his lofty intelligence couldn't grasp this revelation. If a dog got married, why would he move to Oakland? It makes more sense for a married dog, or even one who is just engaged, to avoid the entire Bay Area and settle in a place where no fog obscures the things to chase and his ball won't roll down a two-mile hill.

Not realizing that he was in over his head with this kid, a realization that I also succeed in ignoring, Art pressed on and said, "Now that your dog has gone off to start his own home, do you think you'll be getting another pet?"

"Yes," she said, "a beaver."

"A beaver, eh?" said Art, wishing that he had been wise enough to talk to this girl about something simple, like quantum physics. "Isn't a beaver . . . well, sort of an odd choice for a pet?"

"No, he could sharpen pencils for me."

———

And maybe sharpen Art's mind and mine so that we wouldn't ask questions like the one I gave to a girl of eight.

"Let's see if you know this famous saying," I told her. "A penny saved is . . ."

"One cent," she replied.

I could have gotten that answer from Alan Greenspan, but not when he was eight.

———

Kids look at old sayings, songs, and rhymes in ways so simple that adults cannot, no matter how simple the adult.

"Do you have a favorite nursery rhyme?" I asked one girl of six.

"Yes," she said, " 'Little Miss Muffet.' She sat on a tuffet."

"What's a tuffet?" I said.

"What she sat on."

I will never stop wondering if that girl thought that Miss Muffet's tuffet was an ottoman, a large croissant, or her lower end.

———

Confucius said, "Life is simple. People insist on making it complicated." Confucius must have said this at seven, because kids love to keep it simple.

"What does your daddy do?" I asked a girl of six named Laurie.

"He works on rockets," she said.

KIDS SAY THE DARNDEST THINGS

"Is he an astronaut?"

"No, he's too fat."

"Is he doing anything about it?"

"No, he's on a diet."

Only a child knows that the way not to lose weight is to go on a diet. If any diet really worked, why would there be ninety-seven different ones simultaneously on sale?

———

One girl of five was the essence of simplicity with Art, who asked her, "What does your daddy do?"

"He's a lawyer," she replied.

"Do you know what a lawyer does?"

"Yes, he gets bad people out of jail."

There's probably more money in that than putting good people into jail.

———

I think the one quality in kids that Art and I treasure most is their refusal to put on pretentious airs. You remember that young pilot who, if his engines quit, would use all his aeronautical training to say "Our Father Who art in heaven." Well, in the same rugged tradition is the six-year-old boy I talked to in his karate class.

"Show me the position you take when you're being attacked," I said, and he took it, a stance that was menacing if you were easily menaced.

"Ha!" he cried, and I wondered if he was attacking or laughing at me.

"That's very tough-looking," I said. "You look like Bruce Lee." Actually, he looked more like Kathie Lee, but I still wasn't going to mess with him. "And *now* what do you do?"

"Run," he proudly said.

———

Colleges of agriculture offer courses on such things as milking cows; but a boy of five named Roger gave me the oral Cliffs Notes.

"How do you get milk from cows?" I asked him.

"You pull the sticks," Roger replied.

———

Another agricultural authority, a girl of six named Kate, knew that Roger's knowledge of cows was flawed. She knew that there were no *sticks* under a cow unless some hockey equipment had been left in the barn.

"Do you know how to milk a cow?" I asked her.

"Yes," she replied. "You get a stool and then put your hands way under the cow and pull on the balloons."

"You know, that's also called the udder."

"The other?"

"No, the *udder*. And some people call it the sticks."

———

Because I had never heard of either the sticks or the balloons, I wondered about these sources of milk for a long time. Roger had made the cow sound like a brown hand grenade; Kate had made it sound like a Mardi Gras. And then the whole matter was clarified when I happened to talk farming with another girl of six.

"What's your favorite animal?" I asked her.

"A cow," she replied.

"And do you know where milk comes from?"

"From the A&P."

———

However, where do the people in *Turkey* come from? Maybe from Turkey and maybe not. You may want to return to the herds that are grazing in the A&P after you hear this exchange that Art had years ago with a girl of eight.

151

"Have you studied geography at school?" he asked her, wondering if she might be able to help him with the freeway signs.

"Yes," she replied. "Geography is my favorite subject."

"Wonderful, I love it too. Do you know where Istanbul is?"

"It used to be in Turkey."

"You mean they moved it to Greece?"

"No, you see, the early settlers in Istanbul, well, they thought they were living in Constantinople. It wasn't till many years later that they discovered their mistake."

I wonder if they all had to fill out change of address cards.

———

A kid's sense of time and space would have been appreciated by Einstein—but not in a car.

While going somewhere—crazy, I think—in the car with my children, one of them said, "Are we there yet?"

"No," I told her, "we've got another hour to go."

"But are we *there* yet?" she said, seeing no reason why we hadn't already arrived in both Cleveland and Constantinople.

I wonder if this question is ever used for interrogating prisoners.

KIDS SAY THE DARNDEST THINGS

"If you don't reveal the plans, Lieutenant, I will have to ignore the Geneva Convention and ask you, 'Are we there yet?' "

———

You see, kids think that everything in the world is around the corner from everything else, as Art learned one day when he asked a boy of eight, "Do you know how far away the sun is?"

"Yes," the boy replied. "The sun is ninety-three miles away as the crow flies."

———

This boy will learn, of course, that no crow could take the heat of that trip. He might, however, be able to make it to the moon, a better destination because he could have it for lunch.

"I don't like green cheese," said a girl of seven after I had told her that the moon might be a dairy section of the universe.

"Did you ever eat green cheese?" I said, remembering that phantom broccoli.

"I wouldn't fly all the way to *yellow* cheese either. It's too far to go for yucky stuff."

"You like your yucky stuff to be closer."

"Right."

"Would you ever want to take a ride into space?"

"I don't know. How long does it take?"

Aldrin to Armstrong: *Are we there yet?*

———

When a kid holds forth on geography, it is often a salute to Amelia Earhart.

To one five-year-old boy, I said, "If you couldn't live in the United States, what foreign country would you like to live in?"

"Chicago," he replied.

"Yes, I know people in our embassy there."

———

On a kid's wobbly globe, a visa is needed for Chicago, but London is a state capital.

"Grace, I hear you're from another country," I said to a girl of seven.

"No," she said, "I'm from England."

"What language do they speak there?"

"I think they speak Englandish."

"Can you say something in Englandish?"

"Well, I left when I was very little, so I don't really remember anything."

"I think it would be fun to learn the language they speak in England. I never heard much of it in Philadelphia."

———

On one of his *House Party* shows, Art Linkletter may actually have heard some Englandish from a girl of seven.

"What do you want to be when you grow up?" Art asked her.

"I want to be an octopus," she replied, "so I can grab all the bad boys and spank them with my testicles."

"I think you mean tentacles," said Art, wondering if this conversation was going to be oceanography or pornography.

"That's what I said: My testicles."

"Yes, of course."

And so, Art dropped it there after having been part of a conversation about the first octopus with testosterone.

———

Kids use the language, whether English or Englandish, in delightfully creative ways.

"Can you tell me why we have seasons?" said Art to a girl of six.

"It's because when you bake a cake, that makes it taste better," she replied.

Martha Stewart probably thinks you add vanilla instead of October.

However, a boy of seven on one of my shows had a better grasp of the calendar.

"What are the four seasons?" I asked him.

"Summer, fall, winter, and hay fever," he replied.

Or, as Shakespeare put it: spring, summer, fall, and hockey.

Neither Martha Stewart nor Shakespeare could want more out of life than another girl to whom Art spoke, one who was eight.

"What do you want out of life?" he asked her.

"Right away, I want a rich husband, a Cadillac, and twins," she replied.

"In that order?" said Art, a sentimental man who might have put the Cadillac *after* the twins.

"No," said the girl, "all at once."

"Why do you want those things all at once?"

"To get it all over with."

KIDS SAY THE DARNDEST THINGS

And that thought—original and fearlessly spoken—is typical of the thousands of kids who have shown Art and me that civilization is not necessarily the best way to live.

"If you could change school any way you wished," said Art to a boy of eight, "how would you do it?"

"Tear it down," the boy merrily replied.

There are, of course, other ways to change a school, but none as thorough as that one.

———

Just as boldly original was the mind of a boy of seven, to whom I said, "Do you know the rules of baseball?"

"Oh, sure," he said.

"Okay, what's Rule Fourteen?"

"If you go to the bathroom during a game, you forfeit."

The designated bladder rule.

———

I learned how penetrating the mind of a kid could be when I was a kid myself in Philadelphia. One day, Junior Barnes got his hands on a real boomerang, which he proudly showed to Fat Albert.

"What's *that* thing for?" said Fat Albert, whose substance was everywhere but in his mind.

"You're the biggest moron in Philadelphia," said Junior

Barnes, a statement that would have been hard to chal-
lenge. There were morons as *moronic* as Fat Albert, but
certainly none that was bigger. "This is a broomerang. It's a
magic weapon. You throw it at somebody an' it comes right
back to you."

"*I'm* the moron?" said Fat Albert. "You mean you try to
hit a guy an' you hit *yourself*? Now, *that's* really dumb!"

"Look, they use it in Austria," said Junior Barnes, "so go
ask the Austrianos."

"But it don't make no *sense.* All the enemy gotta do is
follow it back an' they know where you are."

————

Fat Albert, by the way, once told me a darndest thing,
which I have treasured for fifty years. A drugstore in our
neighborhood was having what it called a two-one sale:
You bought an item and received for no charge another of
the same item.

"I just take the free one," said Fat Albert, America's first
insider trader.

————

Here we have two splendid examples of kids trying to think
in 1950, when little of that was being done. As the century
moved on, however, the kids got smarter for Art Linkletter

and even smarter than that for me. I think kids' intelligence may have peaked when a girl of seven recently gave me a look at the scientific wonders that the twenty-first century will bring.

"What's the one great thing that still needs to be invented?" I asked her.

"A roll of toilet paper that never runs out," she replied.

What an intoxicating idea! You receive your one roll of toilet paper as a graduation present and then you are on a roll for life.

———————

Kids think of things like that, just as they think of unique ways to describe themselves.

"How would you describe yourself?" I asked a boy of six.

"A normal boy," he said. "Half in trouble and half out."

"What half is out?"

"When I'm asleep."

"So sometimes you get in trouble at school?"

"Yeah, school is trouble. And they make me go every day."

"What grade are you in?"

"The second, I think."

"You *think*? Haven't you been there enough to notice the door?"

"Yeah, it's probably the second."

"And what are you learning?"

"School stuff."

"Yes, I figured it wasn't submarine warfare. Well, tell me, do you like your teacher?"

"She's kind of strict."

"What is strict?"

"She hates me."

"Oh, I'm sure she treats all the kids the same way."

"Yeah, she hates 'em all."

"I'll bet she helps you to learn a lot of things. Can you remember anything you learned this year?"

"I learned the Pledge of Allegiance."

"Wonderful. Could you recite it for me?"

"I pledge allegiance to the flag of the United States of America, and to the public for which it stands, one nation, invisible, with liberty and justice for all."

"Good, that's a lot of it. If the flag doesn't stand for the public, then for whom? Tell me, what's the hardest thing about school for you?"

"Buttoning my pants."

"Yes, that's why I took zippering as an elective."

KIDS SAY THE DARNDEST THINGS

Like that boy who was half in trouble and half out, other kids also like to divide themselves in original ways.

To a boy of six on *Kids Say the Darndest Things,* I said, "What do you want to be when you grow up?"

"A football player," he replied.

"What position do you want to play?"

"Halfback."

"How would you describe a halfback?"

"Half front, half back."

And after his playing career, he could go on to become a United States Centaur.

———

There is, of course, always some slippage in the intellectual advancement of kids from the time of Junior Barnes's Austrianos to the time of the eternal two-ply roll.

"What should you always do before starting any work with tools?" I asked a boy of five.

"First you get a beer," he said.

And then you hammer your sleeve to the plank.

———

With enough beer, you could build a house. Kids are quite well informed about the housing industry.

"How much does a house cost these days?" I asked one girl of eight.

"Oh, about three thousand dollars, if you want to live in Malibu," she said.

And if you can be happy in a beach birdhouse.

———

Yes, kids have insights into housing beyond those of people who hold mortgages.

"Tell me about your home," I said to a girl of six.

"It has rooms," she said.

"Wonderful. A home without rooms is hard to furnish."

"I have one of them."

"Let me guess which one. Your bedroom."

"I have a bed with a headboard."

"A headboard, eh?"

"Yes, it's for bumping your head."

———

On the same subject—or maybe not; I'm never sure what the subject is when I'm talking to a kid—I was in a discussion about older people, those over ten, with a girl of seven named Marjorie, who suddenly decided to enlighten me about a woman's biological clock—and considerably more.

KIDS SAY THE DARNDEST THINGS

"When people get old," Marjorie said, "they can't bear children and some children can't bear old people either."

————————

Well, Art and I have borne thousands of children and borne them all with endless delight. There's a little kid inside each of us and she is happily bumping her head. She has also been keeping things lively in Art's head and mine.

)